Person to Person

Person to Person

Fieldwork, Dialogue, and the Hermeneutic Method

Barry P. Michrina
CherylAnne Richards

State University of New York Press

Dedicated to The Loyal Order of Hermeneuts

Published by
State University of New York Press, Albany

Printed in the United States of America

For information, address State University of New York
Press, State University Plaza, Albany, N.Y., 12246

Production by E. Moore
Marketing by Bernadette LaManna

Library of Congress Cataloging-in-Publication Data

Michrina, Barry P. (Barry Paul), 1947–
Person to person : fieldwork, dialogue, and the hermeneutic method / Barry P. Michrina and CherylAnne Richards.
p. cm.
Includes bibliographical references and index.
ISBN 0-7914-2833-8 (HC : Acid-free). — ISBN 0-7914-2834-6 (PB : Acid-free)
1. Anthropology—Field work. 2. Anthropology—Methodology.
I. Richards, CherylAnne, 1954– . II. Title.
GN34.3.F53M53 1996
301—dc20 95-8930
CIP

10 9 8 7 6 5 4 3 2 1

Contents

Part III: Advanced Considerations

Prologue to Instructors

In countless college courses from psychology to interpersonal relations time is spent in the first week explaining the nature of the scientific method of analysis. Your students have probably been exposed to this several times. Because there is this systematic method and because it is so ubiquitous in academia, scientific data is seen to be valid, by both students and instructors. Ethnographic data is more suspicious in most circles and is often devalued by being referred to as anecdotal. It is because ethnographic fieldwork has lacked the systematic model used in scientific studies that it has remained suspect. In this book we will present a systematic investigative method called dialogical hermeneutics that we feel will rival the scientific method in its rigor and in its philosophical underpinnings. The word "dialogical" refers to the use of dialogue—dyadic conversation, negotiation of an understanding. The word "hermeneutic" refers to the construction of a description of a whole scene or phenomenon through an incremental analysis of information. Taken together they refer to a method of holistic description through incremental analysis of dialogue.

This text is aimed at undergraduate students in the disciplines of anthropology, sociology, psychology, criminal justice, and journalism. We assume that your students have taken an introductory course in cultural anthropology. We want them to learn how to apply material that heretofore has been largely kept in the academy's ivory towers. We feel optimistic in breaking new ground; we sense that the soil is thirsty for this knowledge.

The hermeneutic method is employed in the humanistic paradigm of anthropology. This paradigm is a collection of perspectives, all of which emphasize understanding other cultures or groups in terms of one human in relation to another (as opposed to humans being explained as objects of research). These include phenomenological, descriptive, and communicative perspectives. The epistemological basis in this paradigm is intersubjective; that is, trying to experience and/or to understand the feelings and thoughts of others, by using one's full human potential: emotions, interpersonal experience, and intellect.

The hermeneutic method can be traced from its 1545 introduction by Martin Luther for biblical interpretation, as coexisting with the Enlightenment tradition and positivism. It was first applied to the social sciences by Vico and was raised to prominence by Dilthey, who emphasized the application of both *erlebnis* (i.e., one's lived experience) and *verstehen* (i.e., empathic understanding) in the method.

Although the hermeneutic method was used implicitly by anthropologists such as Turnbull, it explicitly emerged in anthropology through several channels: Ward Goodenough's ethnoscience, Victor Turner's anthropology of performance, and Clifford Geertz's interpretive anthropology.

Ethnopsychology, a type of ethnoscience, has made special use of this method, as is demonstrated by works of Geoffry White and Catherine Lutz. Turner referred explicitly to Dilthey in applying *erlebnis* and *verstehen* to the ethnographic method. Geertz emphasized the semiotic approach in incorporating hermeneutics into anthropology.

More recently, the dialogical approach of Mikhail Bakhtin has been applied to the hermeneutic method to create a dialogical hermeneutics. James Clifford, George Marcus, and Dick Cushman have emphasized dialogical negotiation and the need to hear "all voices" during fieldwork, and Ian Prattis has introduced a model for dialogical hermeneutics employing anthropological poetics.

Among sociological perspectives the hermeneutic method would appear to us to be applicable to Weber's *verstehen*, to the symbolic interaction of H. G. Mead and Herbert Blumer, to the naturalistic inquiry approach of N. K. Denzin, and to some forms of ethnomethodology. Yvonna Lincoln and Egon Guba have introduced the naturalistic inquiry method to education, while the hermeneutic method has been introduced to psychology by S. Kvale, G. S. Howard, K. J. Gergen, and others. There, it may also be referred to as the constructivist method.

The hermeneutic method cannot be equated with postmodernism, though it interconnects with the movement in several respects. Postmodernists use the metaphor of a text for deconstruction, and hermeneutic analysis has been described as textual interpretation. Also, the hermeneutic method offers descriptions that lie outside the positivist (i.e., scientific) paradigm. Recent emphasis from postmodernist anthropologists concern the dimension of power, authority, and exploitation in doing and writing ethnography. These are also concerns of the hermeneutic method, however, not in the critical sense. To us postmodernism is more critical of modernists and more skeptical about the enterprise of social science. The hermeneutic method has been, and continues to be, an alternative to the scientific method. We do not suggest that this method will displace or transform the scientific method.

Our message here is bold and assertive. We feel that ethnographic analysis has come of age. The hermeneutic method is teachable; it includes a means of validation; and its posture toward the native is humble. Our assertiveness in presenting the method is born from our frustration with the skeptical criticisms of ethnography, with the attempts of ethnographers to make the method appear "scientific" for the sake of funding, and with practitioners' confusion with regard to epistemology.

Preface

We want this manual to provide several options for readers. Some instructors may wish to have students read all of the material first, before beginning any fieldwork. The philosophy of such an approach is that students need to be well-prepared for their first field experience. This preparation conceivably would create good habits, give direction, and allay anxiety.

Other instructors may wish students to begin their fieldwork project within the first week or two of the course. The philosophy in this case is that students learn best by doing. They may have anxieties and may make mistakes, but by getting experience they are better able to grasp and retain the material once they have read it. It is to be hoped that they will recognize the errors made in early attempts as they read the manual throughout the semester.

We prefer a third approach, which has the students learn by reading *and* by making mistakes. Here, reading occurs both before and during initial fieldwork. We've tried to accommodate all three styles in this manual. The first nine chapters are essential to good fieldwork technique. These can be read thoroughly (and in order) for those who wish to be well-prepared before they venture into their projects.

For those who need to get into the field as soon as possible, we suggest quickly reading chapters 1 and 3–8. As the semester progresses, these may be reread more thoroughly along with the unread chapters. The exercises may be done at that time. This is also a good idea for the third option. Helpful hints are provided in the appendix for early guidance and as a reminder of lessons from the chapters.

Acknowledgments

I would like to thank Catherine Lutz for introducing me to the hermeneutic method and for her patience in watching me slowly overcome my reluctance to embrace it.

I have appreciated classroom interaction and other dialogue with the following students: Shirley Rowe, Jodi McIntosh, Vicki Wehrman, Russ Twitchell, Leanna Atkinson, Karena Stocker, Robin Baker, and Ken Steffens. I also greatly appreciate permission to use quotes from the ethnographic essays of Rowe, McIntosh, Baker and Stocker.

I would like to thank my colleagues, Paul Reddin, Karen Gallob, and Tom Graves for their support and encouragement. Also, I am greatful for suggestions made by Jose Peer on the original draft of theory, which led to my use of the word "challenge" to describe the essential step in the method.

I am grateful to HarperCollins, University Press of Kentucky, and Johns Hopkins University Press for granting us permission to print sections of their publications.

Most of all, I would like to acknowledge the effort, cooperation, insight, and excitement that CherylAnne Richards has brought to this project. She has been a student who teaches her teacher.

Barry P. Michrina

PART I

THEORY

Chapter 1

UNDERLYING PHILOSOPHY

The central point of the hermeneutical disciplines consists in a specific kind of self-knowledge, and this point distinguishes them from the natural sciences.
—Hans-Georg Gadamer

Many students cringe at the thought of being taught theory in any discipline. The abstractness is difficult to conceptualize for some students and is difficult to apply to real situations for others. We will try to give you a grounding in real fieldwork situations as we explain the philosophical concepts that underlie the hermeneutic method. Hopefully, you will develop a "feel" for these theories. Your understanding will be deepened in subsequent chapters as we include references to philosophical principles in our descriptions of the practical aspects of fieldwork. We also expect students to be reminded of these philosophical concepts as they do their fieldwork projects—making the concepts more real.

It is our belief that method without theory is weak and indefensible and that theory without method is abstract and aimless. The two belong together and need to be taught together. We would like to introduce this topic by delineating two distinctive paradigms that exist in the social sciences today: the scientific and the humanistic. A paradigm is a major category of perspective, an orientation in thinking, a worldview. By understanding the humanistic paradigm and its distinction from the scientific, you can better grasp the rationale for the hermeneutic method.

We will present this to you in the form of a dialogue between a member of each paradigm (and a user of each method).

SCIENTIST: Those of us whose perspective falls under the scientific paradigm tend to see the social world as consisting of regularities and of laws that apply universally to all social groups. It is the investigators' responsibility to determine these laws and regularities in all their ramifications. They allow us to predict future events. We in this paradigm see the social world as existing objectively. By this I mean that it lies totally outside the mind of the investigator and of the subjects being studied. Just as we can study the chair on which you are sitting by measuring it, noting the material from which it is made, its shape and color, we can also study objective social reality.

HERMENEUT: So you believe that the social world can be studied without bias?

CY: Yes, in fact, the scientist has the responsibility to rid him- or herself of all preconceived notions while gathering the objective, empirical data that can be noted of the outside, social reality. This means that the investigator can, and must, control all prestructured knowledge in his or her mind and all of his or her bias. Likewise, in order to prevent any distortion in the scientist's view of objective reality, he or she must treat all subjects of investigation in exactly the same manner; the investigator should not influence those being studied, nor should the subject influence the scientist's method.

HERMAN: Hmmm. Can you give me an example of theories that are represented by this paradigm?

CY: Well, there is Freud. According to Freud, laws of psychosexual development determine human behavior. By being objective, a Freudian investigator feels able to see reality as it exists free of societal interpretation. For example, the Freudian anthropologist might explain myths, customs, or religious beliefs as culturally created means for group members to displace their *unconscious* internal feelings by interpreting them as occurring in external phenomena. According to this theory, the natives are not conscious of their true feelings and motivations, nor of the true nature of the processes being employed. So, painful male puberty rites might be looked at by Freudians as related to the rivalry between father and son for the sexual attention of the mother. They believe that this rivalry is universal in human males, naming it the Oedipus complex, and that cultures often provide means for its expression and resolution. The natives would not express this explanation.

HERMAN: Okay. I think I understand. Can you give me another example?

CY: Followers of Marvin Harris's theory of cultural materialism would assume that laws of ecological or nutritional dependence dictate cultural practices regardless of the natives' conception of the practices. These theorists believe that universal laws regarding the need for nutrients cause the creation of cultural practices. For Marvin Harris, the sacred cow of India did not arise from purely religious sources (as the natives would say) but because of its usefulness for producing milk and draft power with little overt feeding by the owners. As was the case with Freudian theory, Harris's theory assumes that natives are not likely to be aware of the objective laws and explanations that underlie and give rise to their social behaviors.

HERMAN: I'm curious about how scientists can see objective social reality when the natives so frequently misinterpret it.

CY: We use the scientific method—an exacting, systematic method for explaining social reality.

HERMAN: That sounds like something that a physicist or chemist might use.

CY: Yes, it's basically the same method. We can't control people in the social setting the way the physicist might control his objects of study, so we might not follow the steps in the same rigorous manner. However, we still use the method as a model for investigation.

HERMAN: Hmmm. Those of us whose perspectives best fit within the humanistic paradigm don't presuppose that we can know objective social reality. We think that each group has its shared understanding of reality and that the best we can do is to study their shared understanding. We cannot know things objectively, but rather we know them intersubjectively—as a shared understanding among subjects.

CY: It sounds as if you are looking at an intersubjective truth rather than at objective truth.

HERMAN: That's another way of putting it.

CY: How do you learn about this intersubjective truth?

HERMAN: In order to learn about these shared meanings of social existence the investigator must examine some expression of the shared meaning. Some investigators study and interpret the behavior of the group members. Others feel, however, that the more appropriate data is the discourse of cultural (or social group) members, and in particular dialogue with them. The assumption here is that the investigator must ensure that he or she shares the intersubjective understanding of group members in order to be able to describe it to outsiders. This process involves tearing down one's mental structure or initial understanding through a negotiating dialogue with group members.

CY: What do you do about investigator bias?

HERMAN: According to this perspective, biases can cause conflict that is beneficial in its resolution. On the one hand, this conflict could be internal to the investigator. By this I mean that it could cause him or her to experience cognitive dissonance. On the other hand, it may be external to the investigator, such as a disagreement between the investigator and a group member over who they are. Whatever the character of the conflict, the resolution should lead to a congruent understanding. This is all part of the hermeneutic method, which is an exacting method in the humanistic paradigm. As you mentioned to be the case for the scientific method, the hermeneutic method may frequently be a mere model for the proper conduct of ethnographic investigation, rather than a rigorously adhered-to method. Humanists should seek to follow it as an ideal.

CY: I didn't know that humanist ethnography could be carried out using a stepwise method. Could we take a minute to compare this hermeneutic method with the scientific method?

HERMAN: That's a good suggestion; I appreciate your interest. How do we start?

CY: Let's each draw a diagram for our method and then describe each step in the process. You've probably seen the cycle of the scientific method in sociology or psychology textbooks (see Figure 1.1). In step 1, the investigator generates a hypothesis about how one variable relates to another. This is nearly always based on a currently accepted sociological theory. In step 2, the scientist assigns operational definitions to the variables. In other words, he or she will describe the operations that will be used to measure each variable. In step 3 the scientist chooses a research design, and in step 4 he or she selects an unbiased sample that represents the population of concern. In step 5, the investigator generates data. For example, he or she might administer a survey to the population. In step 6, he or she analyzes the data, often by statistical analysis, and tests the hypothesis. In step 7, the analyses are interpreted in light of the original theory. Then the investigator designs a new hypothesis and the cycle is followed again. The key element in this method is testing the hypothesis. In other words, the scientist tries to disprove a story of how things work. This involves searching for and applying objective measurements for the variables so that the hypothesis can be objectively tested.

HERMAN: That was a clear and concise explanation. Let me see if I can do as well with my diagram. The basic hermeneutic method consists of three steps that are enacted again in a continuous fashion (Figure 1.2). The investigator first gathers data in a stepwise manner from sources such as written texts, dialogues, and behaviors. Then he or she attributes some meaning to the data. This is called interpretation. In the third step, the hermeneut constructs an understanding of the whole group from interpreted pieces of data. With each turn of the cycle the hermeneut adds more and more detail to his or her understanding. We assume that a holistic picture of the cultural members is being constructed through this process. By this I mean that the overall description shapes the interpretation of the next piece of information, and that the interpretation adds detail to the description.

In contrast to the scientific method that you just described, the story is broadened, deepened, and reshaped with each new piece of data. We aren't testing the story in an attempt disprove it. Perhaps the best metaphor for this process is artistry. Like artists, hermeneuts construct a detailed pic-

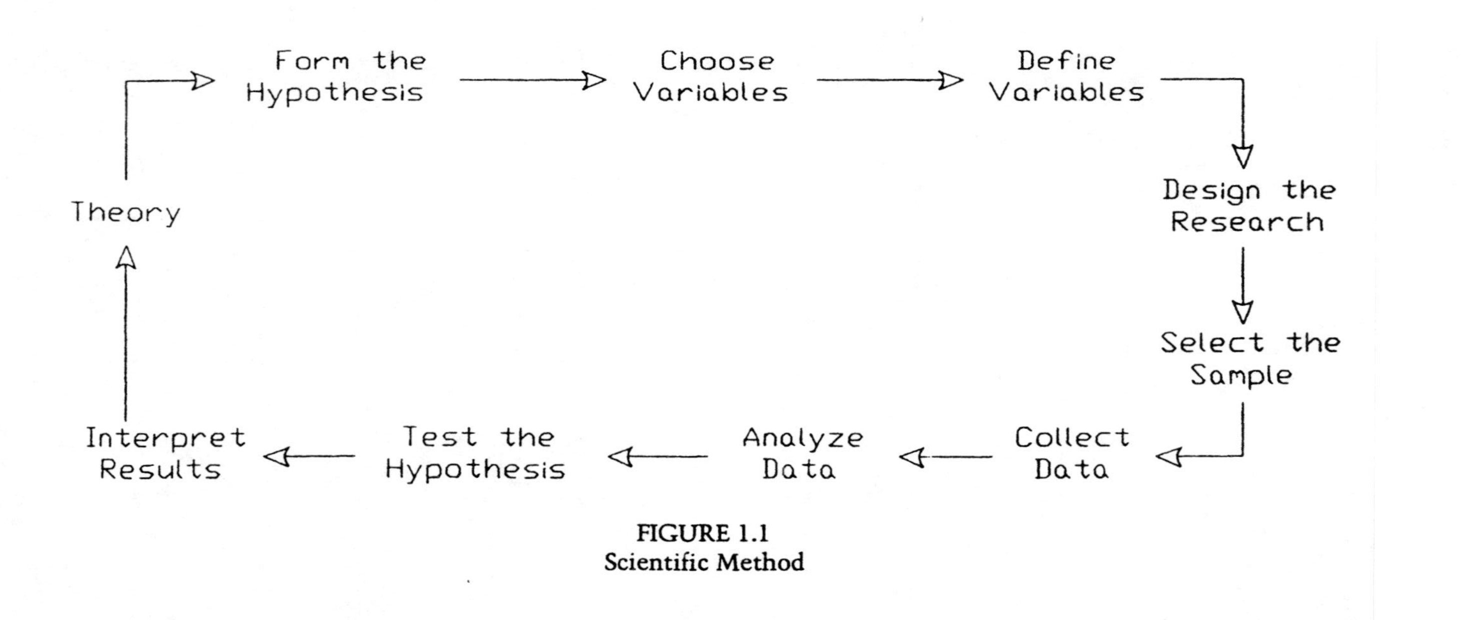

FIGURE 1.1
Scientific Method

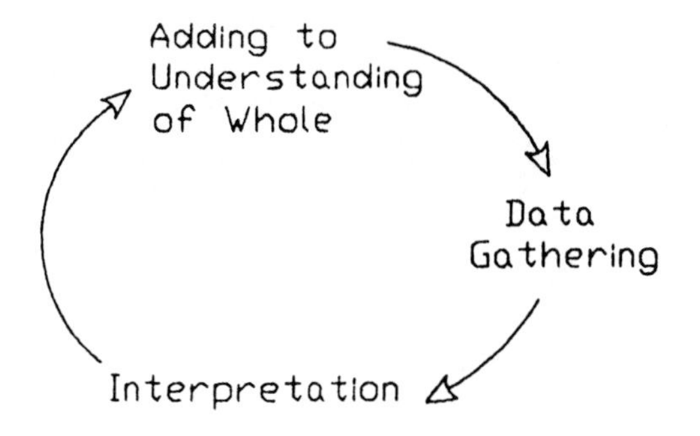

FIGURE 1.2
Basic Hermeneutic Method

ture beginning with rudimentary shapes and adding further refinement and detail with continued rendering. In this respect the process is additive or constructive.

CY: I can see that there is a difference of approach. I don't mean to be rude, but what you just described doesn't have the systematic nature or detail that the scientific method has.

HERMAN: Actually, I'm just getting started. The hermeneutic method includes two detailed models that differ in both procedure and presuppositions. These are the textual hermeneutic model and the dialogical hermeneutic model. The "challenge" is a key feature of both these models, so let me describe it first.

CY: Go ahead. I'll interrupt if I don't follow your explanation.

HERMAN: A "challenge" occurs when a discrepancy arises between the picture or description formulated thus far and a new piece of information. The new information cannot be added comfortably to the current understanding. You may have heard people say that something "does not compute." What they probably meant was that something did not make sense within their current understanding of a situation.

CY: Given what you said about "painting a picture," this challenge sounds like a disaster. Does that mean that all of your fieldwork up to that point will be discredited?

HERMAN: Actually, it represents more of a "eureka" experience—now the investigator can better get at the group members' level of understanding. You see, the big picture now has to be reformulated. While this is time-consuming, the work of reformulation brings one to analyze his or her biases and, in some cases, to enter a negotiating dialogue with informants. The data that you gather after reformulation will either support this new picture or will lead to another challenge. Using the metaphor of the artist, he or she may find at some point that the painting does not properly capture the essence of the subject of interest. Perhaps the perspective or the overall tone is wrong. The artist will then rework the image until a suitable rendition is attained.

CY: I think that I'm following you. Maybe some examples would help me grasp the concept of challenge.

HERMAN: An investigator who grew up in the Nebraska farmlands may think that members of the working class of western Pennsylvania would have values similar to his or her own, that the presence of unions in a region discourages the entry of new business enterprises. One of the group members (we call them informants in anthropology) may say something that is out of character with this picture; for example, "Unions protect the worker." Because this is an expressed value that the investigator hadn't anticipated, a challenge should occur that would lead the investigator to discover that he or she had been using too much of past experience in understanding this informant. This is a form of bias. The field-worker would try to modify his or her understanding to accommodate the unexpected information and then interact further with him or her, keeping a watchful mind for new, unexpected remarks.

Another example I have comes from my own experience. In 1983 I had a stark challenge to my understanding of residents of a substance abuse facility. After agreeing to voluntarily teach and counsel at the center, I began to picture the residents as desperate and violent. My picture became more detailed as I viewed the male, adolescent residents on my trip to interview with the director. Unkempt appearance, tattoos, and loud and crude language fit my picture of a dangerous group. The director talked to me about security procedures and told me that most of the adolescent residents had been sent there by a judge in lieu of prison. This added more detail to the picture that I had already painted. I found even more supporting evidence when I reported for my first evening of teaching; the dining hall was filled with a raucous group. Then I experienced new evidence that challenged the picture I had been forming. The students whom I taught were very eager to please me. They seemed very innocent and childlike. I was forced to reformulate my picture of these students as dangerous, and I found myself examining my biases concerning drug users, unkempt and tattooed adolescents, and the attitude of the supervisor.

By the way, I need to point out that the challenge step in the hermeneutic method is different than the other challenges that the project may present to investigators. Talking to strangers about their lives may be a challenge, but this is not the challenge step in hermeneutics.

CY: This notion of challenge makes sense to me. I'm eager to hear how it fits into the two models that you mentioned earlier.

HERMAN: With the textual model, the investigator gathers data as if the culture were an unchangeable text to be read. This model works well for studies of archival data, archaeological data, or of observed ritual behavior or interpersonal interaction. Have you ever heard of ethnomethodology? It's a specific type of theory and method in sociology. People who practice it observe people's behavior and interpret it while maintaining as unobtrusive a position as possible. They may overhear conversations among group members but seldom enter into them. For them, the social scene appears to be an unchanging text. For all three cases that I've mentioned here, the investigator collects data, interprets it, and adds it to a whole description in a piece-by-piece fashion (see Figure 1.3). When discrepant data occurs, it causes a challenge to arise. The challenge requires that the investigator go through a secondary loop in which he or she analyzes biases in a process called reflexion. Note that the word is spelled with an *x*.

CY: With an *x*?

HERMAN: It means more than reflection with a *ct*. Reflexion requires one to contemplate the cultural, political, and personal biases that led to the errant description. By personal biases I'm referring to psychological biases. Once he or she is aware of how these biases may have led to an improperly drawn

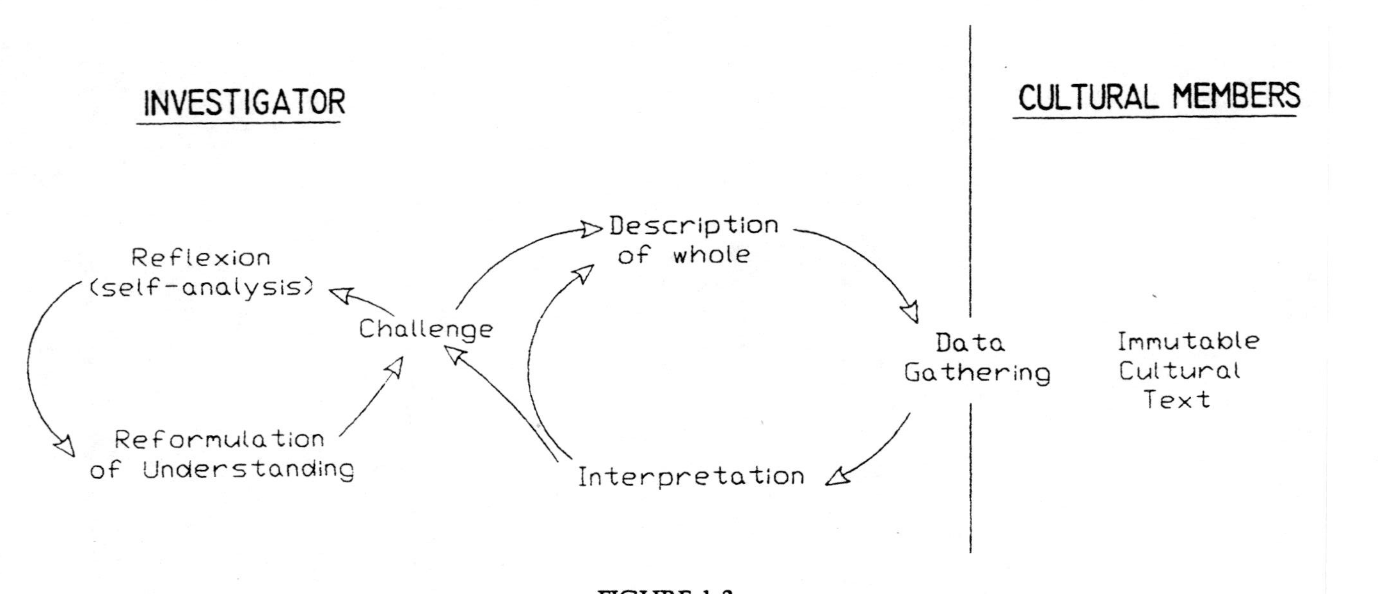

FIGURE 1.3
Textual Hermeneutic Method

picture, the investigator is able to reformulate the description, including all the data gathered thus far. Thereafter, the investigator follows the basic additive cycle until another challenge occurs.

CY: I can see now what you meant when you mentioned earlier that bias acts as a signal to the investigator. What about the dialogical model?

HERMAN: In the dialogical model, dialogue between group members and the ethnographer represents the best source of data. Other sources include other discourse such as overheard conversations, poems, speeches, fictional writing, or song lyrics. Dialogical methodologists consider these to be expressions of an evolving intersubjective understanding, in other words an evolving culture. Followers of this model do not see culture as an immutable text.

There are more loops added to the basic cycle (see Figure 1.4). First of all, there is a reflective branch added because interpretation sometimes requires time for the hermeneut to digest the information. This reflection may include some considerations of the context under which the discourse was created. For example, an investigator might ask how the cultural member viewed the situation in which he or she created the discourse—Was it meant as humor rather than a serious statement? The reflection could also include analysis of the process by which the analyst obtained it. This model includes the rudimentary additive cycle and separate paths necessitated by a challenge to the description. Of course, the challenge step has been added to the rudimentary cycle. Arrows indicate that the sources of challenge can be interpretations of discourse and interpretations of observations. In other words, an investigator may see or hear something that he or she interprets as incongruous with the current understanding. These challenges are solved in two possible fashions: (1) by reflection—that's with a *ct*—followed by reinterpretation or (2) by reflection or reflexion followed by dialogue and reformulation of the description.

CY: Excuse me, but I'm not sure I follow.

HERMAN: Let me explain further. An example of the first type of resolution would be for the investigator to think about the con-

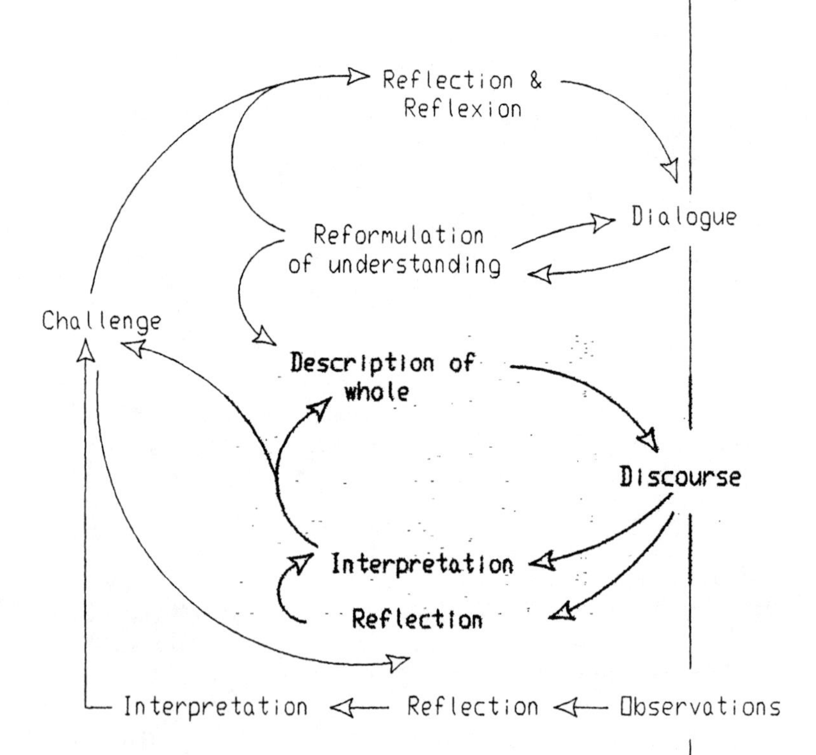

FIGURE 1.4
Dialogical Hermeneutic Method

text in which he or she observed or heard something. What appeared to be a challenge may be understandable with minor expansion of the current description. The second type of resolution requires reflexion by the investigator prior to dialogue, checking for his or her cultural, political, or psychological biases. Bias may have given rise to the challenge and subsequent need for dialogue. As I mentioned before, the biases need to be explored and relaxed for appropriate interpretation to occur.

CY: That sounds like your description of the resolution of challenge for the textual model. Am I right?

HERMAN: Yes, it is very much the same. Since close interaction with people is involved, it might involve more psychological bias. I'll tell you more about this later. I'll describe the second sort of resolution of bias now. It involves negotiation with the informant or informants through dialogue. This negotiation cycle can involve many reformulation steps and several reflection/reflexion steps before the investigator is ready to alter the description of the whole. The dialogue may involve one or more people in one or more conversations. It may occur during one sitting or may require weeks or months.

The resolution cycle may take place many times before the investigator feels prepared to reformulate the overall description. Following the reformulation, the investigator will again interpret the data and add it to the overall understanding until another challenge occurs.

CY: Could you give me an example using this method?

HERMAN: Are you familiar with Richard Lee's article, "Eating Christmas in the Kalahari"? It is a good illustration of the processes involved in dialogical hermeneutics.

CY: I've read it but not recently—refresh my memory.

HERMAN: In his narrative Lee tells of his efforts to present his !Kung informants with an ox for their "Christmas" celebration as a goodwill gesture. He sought the largest, meatiest ox available for slaughter. To Lee's surprise, the !Kung commented unfavorably about his gift. They laughingly referred to it as a bag of bones. When the slaughtered animal proved to be layered with prized fat, Lee was puzzled. The natives still laughed at his "meager" gift. Feeling that something important had gone wrong in his relationship with the !Kung, he asked a Tswana man who had married into the !Kung culture about it and was told that this was customary even among themselves. The hunter's kill was always ridiculed. He then questioned his !Kung informants who told him that they acted this way to prevent arrogance in the provider. They feared that should pride remain the man will someday kill another.

The ridiculing behavior of the !Kung presented a "challenge" to Lee's understanding of them. He resolved the discrepancy between behavior and expectations by reflecting on the situation and on his biases, and by entering into a dialogue with the !Kung. He finally was able to match his horizon or understanding with theirs and to reformulate his description of their culture. He became a part of their circle of shared understanding. In other words, he became able to describe their intersubjective truth.

CY: It seems to me that the most significant difference between the scientific and hermeneutic methods lies in the way their practitioners perceive truth.

HERMAN: Yes, and from that difference flows differences with regard to handling bias, validating stories, and controlling aspects of the investigation. But let's start with epistemology.

CY: The scientific method rests on the assumption that there exists an objective social reality that can be reproducible measured in time and by different investigators. These social phenomena exist "out there," free of investigator bias and investigator interference. Scientists feel that they can categorize and explain social phenomena and even predict them by means of cause-and-effect relationships that some people call laws. For example, cohabitation would be considered an objective phenomenon that can be objectively measured with regard to a variable like years of college education. It does not matter to the scientist that the term "cohabitation" may not be a part of most people's vocabulary, and that the meaning of the live-in relationships may vary widely among those experiencing such practices.

HERMAN: In contrast, the hermeneutic method rests on the assumption that reality cannot be known objectively, but is understood intersubjectively. This means that knowledge of reality is shared among group members. This is their truth. However, it may vary from the truth of another group. The group members create a meaning for what they experience. According to practitioners of the hermeneutic method, truth varies to some extent with time, individual participants, and individual investigators.

CY: That difference in epistemology must have ramifications elsewhere, for example with regard to bias. We espousing the scientific method feel that investigator bias is a preconceived notion that interferes with or distorts taking a measurement of the objective social reality. To us, bias can and must be controlled. We believe that some sort of objective measuring technique must be used to prevent the investigator from distorting the data. An example of such a technique might be survey forms, administered to each participant in exactly the same manner. The investigator usually attempts to distance him- or herself from individuals being investigated. He or she carries this out to control both investigator bias and any deleterious effect that the investigator might have on the responses of the individuals being studied. How do hermeneuts conceptualize bias?

HERMAN: Contrary to what you just described, the supporters of hermeneutics feel that a totally unbiased appraisal of people in the study group is impossible and that the controlled and distant interaction used by scientists in the effort to control bias is undesirable. Rather, they use bias as a detection device. As I mentioned earlier, bias leads to "challenges" to understanding and subsequently to new understandings. Hermeneuts who follow the dialogical model believe that intersubjective truth must be understood through the communication of the investigator with the people being studied; together they must negotiate the understanding that the investigator eventually describes. For example, the investigator trying to understand coal miners might ask an informant: "Would you help clear up something for me? I was under the impression that coal miners realized the dangers under which they were required to work, but you're telling me that you and your fellow mine workers took the responsibility for your own safety. I'm confused." And the investigator might then make more clear his or her sense of contradiction in the statement: "Wouldn't the men hold the company responsible for at least some of the conditions that they had to endure?" A plausible reply by the miner might be: "Only if they were trying to get away with not meeting government regulations." This still might not satisfy the investigator, so he or she might ask: "Do government regulations really provide for a safe workplace?" The informant might reply: "Not entirely, but I say that mining can't be done without some injuries and even deaths." This negotiation of what is considered true for this informant, and possibly for most members of his or her group, would continue until the investigator shed his or her own biases about mine danger and understood the thinking of the informant. This type of process indicates a power relationship that does not exist for the scientific method or for the textual model of hermeneutics.

CY: What type of power relationship are you talking about?

HERMAN: The dialogical hermeneut often finds him- or herself in an equal or inferior position with regard to power since he or she must negotiate what is real with the informant. In contrast, the scientist is in a superior position in exercising the power to treat the subjects of his or her study in an objective manner. The scientist attempts to treat them in a detached manner, as if they were data. Those being studied are relatively powerless with regard to interpersonal relations. Hermeneuts, in their interpersonal relations must often argue with, cajole, seek help with, and reflect understanding back to their informants.

CY: And the textual hermeneuts—where do they fit in?

HERMAN: Hermeneuts using the textual model fall somewhat in-between the scientists and the dialogical hermeneuts. Since they do not negotiate the meaning of reality with their informants they are in a superior power position. They make the interpretations without consulting group members. However, if they are doing participant-observation, they need to please group members as a means of maintaining access to the group. In this sense they treat group members in a less detached manner and have less power.

There is a secondary difference with regard to power. The proponents of the scientific method, and to a large extent the proponents of the textual model of hermeneutics, are elitist in their conclusions.

CY: Excuse me for interrupting, but I don't like the label "elitist."

HERMAN: I only mean to refer to the drawing of conclusions, not to an overall attitude or character. I mean that well-trained social scientists constitute an elite group who have the power to decide what is going on in objective reality (or in the intersubjective understanding of reality of group members for the case of textual hermeneuts). The self-description of those being studied is generally not sought, and is considered irrelevant. In contrast, dialogical hermeneuts must not exercise the power to define the world for other individuals. They must seek dialogue with their informants and through this procedure negotiate an understanding. In this case, the people exercise the power to define themselves. This method requires the investigator to assume a humble posture.

CY: I can see your point. I'll try to not take it as a derogatory adjective. What else do we need to discuss?

HERMAN: We should compare means of validation. How do investigators know if their analysis is valid?

CY: In the scientific method this is brought about through a process called replication. Since followers of the scientific method assume that reality can be objectively determined, they feel that results obtained in one study should be validated by reproducing them in subsequent, identical studies. If you keep getting the same data, it is considered valid.

HERMAN: With regard to the textual hermeneutic model, the validity of the study is determined by the coherence of the description. In other words, the more consistent the description, the more valid. Validation for the dialogical hermeneutic model involves the process of assuring that the investigator's description matches the group's understanding. The assumption here is that it is the group members' shared understanding, so they ought to be able to recognize when an analysis is valid.

The hermeneut needs to validate his or her description through ongoing dialogue and negotiation of understanding with informants. The investigator must articulate his or her current understandings to the informants for comment, refinement, or correction. In essence, the investigator must ask: "Do I have this right?," "Can you tell me more?," and "Can you make it more clear to me?" This validation may occur as an ongoing process during interviews or conversations with the informants. Another means of validation involves asking informants to comment on a written description of the investigator's understanding.

CY: Could you give me a little more detail? It is very different than validation in the scientific method.

HERMAN: In the case of negotiation during interviews, the investigator asks the informant for verification of on-the-spot interpretations. This can include the hermeneut's rephrasing of what he or she thinks the informant is saying or can involve his or her articulating what appears to be implicit meaning within what the informant expressed explicitly. It might also involve asking informants to refine their explanations or descriptions. What ensues during the engagement of serious interviewing is an interaction between two people who react in relation to each other and reciprocally influence each other. The questions and statements of one person can cause the other to reflect on and analyze issues in new ways and perhaps to react emotionally to what is said or the manner in which it is said. Validation may also occur during subsequent interviews when the investigator asks the informant to comment on the interpretations from information provided in the previous conversation.

For example, a negotiation could involve the interpretation of ethnic poetry (or lyrics) by an anthropologist. He or she would present this interpretation to one or more culture members to verify the interpretation. The informant(s) might disagree with the analysis, pointing out errors in understanding. After considering this, the investigator might come back to make certain that his or her new interpretation is that shared by the informants. When informants agree with the interpretation, it would be validated. Again, correction and elaboration become part of the negotiation process. In carrying out negotiations, it is proper to guide the informant toward certain issues or themes, but not toward specific opinions about those issues.

The most comprehensive form of validation of understanding occurs when written material is presented to informants for comment. These manuscript drafts have been designed to express descriptions with a precision greater than that which characterizes conversations. Also, they indicate a sense of permanence. Such qualities may move informants to more carefully consider the validity of what has been expressed. Their comments may lead to further negotiation, to revision and to a final validation.

Table 1.1 summarizes the comparison among the three methods. We hope that this comparison of the analytical methods helps you to see how hermeneutics is distinct in its philosophical basis. In the next chapter we will detail the characteristics of the hermeneutic method. Remember, each time that we address the characteristics of the hermeneutic method it will become more clear to you. Even in later chapters as we describe the fieldwork procedures, we will be again addressing these philosophical principles.

TABLE 1.1
Comparison of Methods

	Scientific	*Textual Hermeneutic*	*Dialogical Hermeneutic*
Epistemology	objective	intersubjective/ subjective	intersubjective
Bias	controllable	tool (challenge)	tool (challenge and dialogue)
Power	with investigator	with investigator	with informants
Validation	replication	coherence	verification by informants

EXERCISES

1.1 Define the following words based on descriptions in this chapter: trust, challenge, reflexion, understanding, negotiations, reformulation, description, dialogue, and intersubjective truth.

1.2 Write a short essay based on your understanding of chapter 1: Can a person carry out a heremeutic study if the informants don't believe in intersubjective truth, but rather in one objective truth that they have figured out? Why or why not?

1.3 Draw the diagram for the dialogical hermeneutic method, explaining why the two arrows lead into description and one comes out. Tell why the two arrows lead into challenge and the two arrows come out.

Chapter 2

Theoretical Principles

. . . anthropological knowledge may be seen as something produced in human interaction, not merely "extracted" from naive informants who are unaware of the hidden agendas coming from the outsider.

—Nancy Scheper-Hughes

We hope that you have gained some appreciation for the difference between the scientific method and the hermeneutic method of analysis. We also hope that you sense the difference in the two models of the hermeneutic method. In this chapter we will leave the scientific method behind and address in more detail the issues of power, bias, epistemology, and validation in the hermeneutic method.

Power

The ethnographer places him- or herself in a "one-down" position in trying to obtain an understanding from informants. The investigator is like a student seeking to learn—a person who seeks knowledge from those who have it. As a relationship of trust builds, the relationship may become more symmetrical in power—the investigator and the informant trying to control the timing of conversations, the topics chosen, and the tone. Kevin Dwyer has published a collection of eleven interviews with a Moroccan *faqir* (a member of a Muslim brotherhood of privileged religious status) recorded in the summer of 1975. These show how each member of the dialogue asserted his own power. Dwyer chose a topic for each dialogue, and insistently delved for answers to his questions. Dwyer saw the *faqir's* power in his digressions, evasions, and termination of the interview. The *faqir* usually ended the session by saying "close that up now" and once fell asleep.

Given that the investigator most often must produce a report for academic promotion (most are degree-seeking graduate students), the threat of loss of an informant also puts the investigator in a "one-down" position. This makes the hermeneutic analysis a humble enterprise. Both members in the conversation may realize the precariousness of the analyst's position. The field-worker does not have the power to command cooperation and reliability from the informant; it comes with the building of a trusting and respectful relationship. What this means is that the entire report is a product of a series of negotiations; first for cooperation and then for understanding.

Since the epistemology of hermeneutic analysis is intersubjective in nature, the understanding that a hermeneut attains should be the result of negotiation with informants. If the investigator thinks he or she understands an issue, the investigator must determine if the understanding will continue to make sense during further conversations on the topic. The ethnographer may ask the informant to confirm or refine his or her current description. This negotiation again demonstrates the power that the informant holds.

There are three areas, however, in which the field-worker usually has all of the power: choice of informants, ownership of data, and writing of the final report. In contrast, there are instances where the investigator is helpless; for example, a potential informant may show disinterest in talking, a key informant may be selective in providing new contacts, or the culture may hold certain interactions as taboo.

When the investigator exerts his or her power in choosing informants, he or she must make certain that all voices are heard, and that his or her choice of informants is truly representative of each group. So, someone studying U.S. voter sentiments must make certain that groups such as Republicans, Democrats, Independents, males, females, the young, the middle-aged, the elderly, rural residents, urban residents, and so on are represented among his or her informants. And in choosing these informants he or she must find people whose statements represent the thoughts of most members of that group.

What of the ownership of the subsequent data? Need it necessarily be controlled by the investigator? Light and Kleiber made their field notes open to all members of the women's health cooperative that they were studying. In this case the members, which included the investigators, wished to share the power to own the data. The very nature of the cooperative dictated this sharing. The hermeneutic method would allow for such a solution with regard to epistemology; after all, if meaning is shared, developed, and negotiated within a group, why should the data that leads to an understanding of this data not be shared as well? However, there may be logistical, political, and cultural problems with such a sharing process. In dispersed populations (for example, Barry's[1] coal-mining families were dispersed over a 2,000-square-mile area) or with short-term studies such as those that most of you will experience in your undergraduate training, the sharing of data with informants is very problematic. Trust is required in this process, and in some cases factions may exist within a population that would lead them to distrust certain people with their open statements. Furthermore, groups sometimes are small enough that anonymity may not be maintained with coding; that is, some members may recognize others despite the coding. Cultural impediments could also inhibit informants from speaking openly about certain topics, if they are going to be read by fellow group members.

Some have argued that there could be an epistemological problem with sharing data among all members of the group. These critics fear that people will be inhibited in telling all the truth about a situation when they know that their acquaintances will be reading it. We feel that a strong trust must exist among group members, and between group members and the investigator, for such sharing to produce useful data.

Similar arguments concerning power could be voiced by informants with regard to the writing of the report. The way data are portrayed, the style and tone of the analysis, as well as generalities and conclusions can lie outside the control of the investigated group. All of this is part of the description of the group's culture. Here again, the hermeneut is in a position to lay bare the information since the negotiation of truth is a characteristic of the method. Barry's solution to the issue of power in writing is one alternative to consider. In his study of coal miners and their wives he gave copies of chapter drafts to key informants for their comments. In one case they objected strongly to an interpretation, leading him to include a reformulated understanding as a separate chapter. He found that this evaluation process helped the key informants to feel as if they were a part of the project. Sharing the power in this process is also respectful to those whose very lives and thoughts are to be bared for public scrutiny.

EPISTEMOLOGY

The use of the hermeneutic method in fieldwork has led to an evolution of the definition of truth in ethnographic studies. Increasingly, ethnographers have placed an emphasis on dialogue in understanding the interpersonal sharing of culture. If a group's shared understanding is sought, then two situations of negotiation of meaning need to be addressed: the process of understanding taking place when natives communicate to, teach, and try to understand one another and the process of understanding that takes place when the ethnographer questions group members. Cultural understanding is what we label "a horizon of understanding." It is a group's view of the world—a view that provides cohesion and distinguishes it from other groups. Is this an evolving understanding? Do the ethnographer's questions stimulate new considerations and new interpretations of their world?

We feel that the answer to both of these questions is "yes," and we have taken into consideration the native's own process of understanding that we have illustrated in Figure 2.1. We show a hermeneutic cycle of the group members. The basic cycle involves reflection on their current culture and worldview. As the investigator asks questions, the informants must reflect on their understanding in a new way. This process is likely to deepen, broaden, or otherwise alter their understanding of themselves. Should they take these same questions or the new understanding to other cultural members they may create a new shared understanding of themselves as a group. Group members' awareness of their awareness of reality will be expanded as they reflect on questions posed by the hermeneut. This aspect of negotiation entices informants to become more conscious of their comprehension of reality as they try to articulate what have been implicit understandings.

We are not upset with the possibility of this investigator effect on the subjects. We consider this to be a natural part of the process of

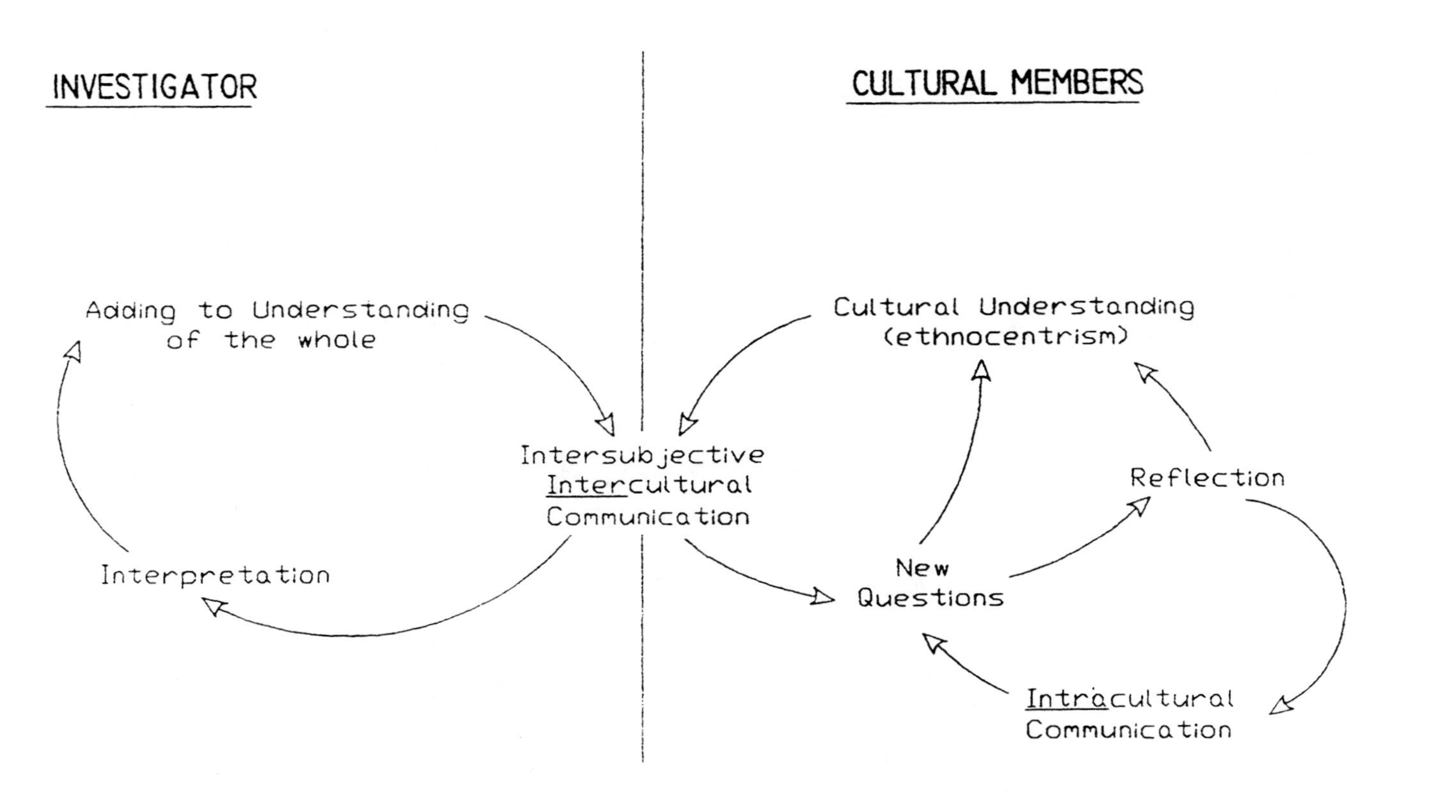

FIGURE 2.1
The Effects of the Investigator on Cultural Members

understanding someone different from ourselves. It means, however, that the study will not be entirely reproducible. The studies are a function, not only of the particular investigator, his or her biases and communication skills, but also of the group members' communication skills: reflecting, intracultural communication (i.e., communication between members) and intercultural communication (i.e., communication between cultures). Even when excluding interaction with anthropologists, a group's shared understanding evolves. In this respect there is not one monolithic rendition of a group's intersubjective understanding that can represent the group for all times or that is free of the effects of human interaction. The factor here that saves this ethnographic process from seeming pointless is a rich and thick description that provides insights through the interaction of investigator with informants and that describes the context of the study. As we mentioned earlier, all voices should be allowed to speak—no group should be ignored. For example, elders may have a worldview different from youths; males different from females. Therefore, one age or one sex should not speak for both sexes or all ages. With all this description we may reach some deeper understanding of the people and of their understandings.

It is the "challenge" and subsequently the reformulation of the whole description following dialogue with informants that yields the intersubjective truth that the hermeneut seeks. Philosopher Hans-Georg Gadamer has suggested that the negotiation involves a matching of horizons between the investigator and those investigated. As an investigator you have a horizon, that is, a set of cultural and personal categories and values, and you will formulate an understanding based to a certain extent on them. Values tell a person what it is that his or her culture prefers, what is allowed, rejected, or is forbidden; they indicate what is beautiful, good, fun, helpful, distasteful, bad, boring, or destructive. Categories indicate the most important qualities of things. For example, occupations are categories of people as are categories of sex and economics. In effect, you will impose these on the informants' explanations—in your lines of questions, in what you unconsciously choose to hear, in how you analyze what you take as data.

If you are lucky and sensitive to a "challenge," one will occur when something an informant says, or does, confronts your understanding of the group's worldview. Your horizon (i.e., categories and values) doesn't match theirs. When this happens, you would have to reformulate your understanding in order to make your horizon align with theirs. Questioning the informants is the best way to achieve this. This dialogical process of matching horizons, or resolving challenges, is what we refer to as "negotiating truth." It involves refined communication skills and the humility characteristic of a power position below or equal in level with the informants. An additional element in this negotiation of understanding is the acknowledgment of bias.

Bias

Bias is a concept indicating the categories and values of one's horizon. We all have cultural, political, and personal biases—they constitute the structure of our worldview. It would be convenient to be able to drop all this structure for the sake of our study and listen with a completely blank mind to what informants have to say, but this is impossible. We need our enculturated worldview in order to germinate an understanding of the world, including the culture of others. The plantlike understanding that emerges may be misshapen and in need of pruning or shaping, but as long as its roots hold onto some substrate it can exist and be manipulated. The source of our empathy, as well as our biases, lies in our prior experiences, understandings, and worldview.

How do we prevent this substrate, this horizon, this bias, from leading to a misunderstanding of the natives? Reflexion is the key. This is a radical self-analysis, a constant vigilance, skepticism, and questioning with regard to one's self. This process is aided by journal-keeping, a technique which can help you keep track of preconceived notions, feelings, formulated pictures of the other culture, your emotional tie to research topics and issues, power struggles, and "challenges." The ability to see some of your biases before, and as a consequence of, challenges will help you to define the natives in their terms.

Individual bias includes one's individual tastes, unique life experiences, and unique emotional transference. If one can't imagine liking weather where the temperatures reach fifty degrees below zero (Fahrenheit); if one doesn't know what it feels like to ride a horse; if one feels that an informant is trying to control him or her because the informant seems "parental," then he or she may have to examine his or her individual biases. Political biases involve power. Does the ethnographer think that he or she can recognize exploitation or dominance independently of what informants tell him or her? Cultural biases might include one's sense that polygamy is wrong, that healing by spiritual power is impossible, that wrongdoers must be punished, or that social classes exist in all societies.

Several investigators have suggested that even psychological transference may involve culturally shaped interpretations more than they represent psychological universals. Here we are defining transference as an emotional, and often cognitive, distortion of reality in which an individual interprets a current relationship as if it were an emotion-laden relationship from childhood. An example of a culturally shaped transference experienced by Barry in his fieldwork was his sense of anxiety about finding a job. In that case he sensed that people worried for him, made suggestions of where to look for work, and gave him the feeling, even early in his fieldwork, that tragedy would befall him if he didn't quickly find full-time, secure employment. He became so caught up in this transference of panic that he frantically sought jobs beneath his training and ability. In the culture of the Appalachian working class where Barry was reared, anxiety related to a person's childhood experiences could be restimulated by the threat of permanent unemployment. However, his feelings might be totally misunderstood in many other cultures. Thus, transference may be looked at as a culturally shaped emotional bias. You may read more of our ideas on this topic, as it relates to lived experience, in chapter 10.

There are two keys to hermeneutic understanding of intersubjective truth: empathy and reflexion. Without empathy we cannot put ourselves in the skin of the other—cannot feel what the other feels, imagine what the other thinks. Without reflexion we are likely to project our own feelings, imaginings, and cognitive structures onto our perceptions and interpretations of the behaviors and explanations of the informant, not seeing the other but rather ourselves reflected back to us.

Validation

How do we know when we are reading a study that validly represents the people of the author's concern? Validation is the process of assuring that the investigator's description matches the group's understanding of reality. There are two modes of validation for the dialogical hermeneut. The foremost of these is affirmation from informants. This can take place at any time during the study: an investigator could question a picture that is forming in his or her mind as an interview unfolds; the investigator could reflect on an interview or analyze it to get a sense of an informant's understanding before questioning the same informant or another to see if this understanding is valid; or the investigator could take the manuscript drafts to informants for validation. In the case of negotiation during interviews, the investigator asks the informant for verification of on-the-spot interpretations. This can include the hermeneut's rephrasing of what he or she thinks the informant is saying or can involve his or her articulating what appears to be an implicit meaning within what the informant expressed explicitly. It may also involve asking informants to refine their explanations or descriptions. What ensues during the engagement of serious interviewing is an interaction between two people who react in relation to each other and reciprocally influence each other. This is a reciprocal cognitive (and at times emotional) influence. The questions and statements of one person cause the other to reflect on and analyze issues in new ways and perhaps to react emotionally to what is said.

Validation may also occur during subsequent interviews when the investigator asks the informant to comment on the interpretations from information provided in the previous conversation. Again, correction and elaboration become part of the negotiation process.

It is important to present the subsequent feedback to readers so that they, in turn, have some sense of the validity of the study. In our opinion feedback from readings of manuscript drafts is the most important source of validity. The material is generally coherent, logically presented, and complete; the informant can take time in reading and reflecting on the draft before commenting; and people feel genuinely involved. The subsequent inclusion of the natives' revisions or the ethnographer's reformulations is particularly symbolic of taking the informants seriously; and they, more than anyone, recognize this. We have found that people generally want to be understood.

The ethnographer is in effect asking: "Am I understanding you correctly? If not, could you help improve my understanding?" It is important for the dialogical hermeneut to keep in mind that the group being studied is not a text, is not a phenomenon to be experienced, and is not something that exists solely in the investigator's mind. In other words, the truth that hermeneuts seek is not objective or subjective. It is an intersubjective truth requiring a dialogical interaction with informants.

Incidently, the hermeneut should not check informants' behavior to see if it matches their discourse. If such discrepencies occur as a natural process of interaction, then the informant should be given the opportunity to explain what the outsider saw as a discrepency.

A second method is to include in the ethnography the details of the challenges and of the reflexive analyses that occurred during the fieldwork. We would find fieldwork that had been done without several major challenges to be either of questionable validity or of questionable value. Readers need to know how the investigator struggled with his or her biases in the processes of challenge and reformulation.

Validation can benefit the reader in two ways: it can inform the reader that dialogical negotiation with informants has occurred, and it can indicate to the reader that the ethnographer has performed reflexive analysis.

The Mothering Metaphor

Whether it is based on personal experience or intuition, some students seem to be able to grasp the "big picture" of hermeneutics easily, while others struggle with it. Some find that the fundamentals of hermeneutics—the participant-observation, self-analysis for bias, continuous reformulation of ideas, and goal of a negotiated and shared understanding—constitute the way in which they *naturally* interact with people who they care about. For these students, a study of hermeneutic principles seems to validate intrapersonal and interpersonal practices with which they are already familiar. In this chapter, we would like to offer a metaphor for the hermeneutic method of social research, one that we believe captures much of the essence of hermeneutic interaction. Hermeneutics is like good mothering.

Like every metaphor, this one has its limitations. There are many ways in which hermeneutics and mothering differ. Mothering involves socialization, which is never the intent of anthropology. A mother is in a position of power and authority, which is an inappropriate position for the hermeneutic ethnographer. The mother is perceived to be superior in intellectual, emotional, and spiritual development, a view that must not be carried into the informant–field-worker relationship. A child "belongs" in a sense to his or her mother, and this does not translate into hermeneutic anthropology. What do these limitations leave us? We are left then to examine the communication and negotiation for understanding between individuals—mother and child—who participate in this negotiation as equals, that is, a "peer" relationship based on the recognition of the absolute value of each individual and their subjective realities.

Keeping these limitations in mind, we will now attempt to show you how hermeneutics *is* like good mothering. Perhaps we would have been more "politically correct" to use the term "good parenting," but our purpose here is to draw an analogy between the immersion aspect of ethnographic fieldwork (and the understanding that this type of experience can foster) and the traditional role of mother as the primary caretaker, participant, and observer in the child's life. Many points of comparison may apply to fathers also, but for the sake of simplicity and continuity, we will use the terms "mother" and "mothering" throughout.

Although the hermeneutic method relies primarily on dialogue, participant-observation can be an important aspect of fieldwork. It is essential to good mothering. As the mother interacts with her infant, she is learning her baby's "language"—just like a field-worker in a foreign culture—and enters his or her world through imitative expressions and sounds. The nonverbal interaction may seem meaningless, but mother and infant are indeed communicating and learning about each other, so much so that many mothers learn to distinguish a hungry cry from a cry of discomfort, pain, or tiredness. We believe that the hours logged in observation alone account for the maternal bond that many find so mysterious. It is as though the hundreds of hours a mother spends gazing at her infant or watching her small child (children *are* the only people we can stare at without violating a social norm!) are hours spent in unconscious data gathering. The data may never be *consciously* compiled, categorized, or analyzed, yet it leads to the mother's ability to "spontaneously" interpret her child's behavior, based not on "mother's instinct," but grounded in the in-depth, ongoing "study" of her own child.

As the infant matures, there are countless ways to enter into his or her world, anything from the shared enthusiasm in rolling a ball back and forth across the floor, to elaborate games of imagination. For example, consider a four-year-old girl who is playing "day care" at home—she is the teacher, and her dolls, stuffed toys, and mother are the "kids." By refraining from directing the playtime in any way (except to play her role), the mother is given the opportunity to observe her *daughter's* perception of day care. Any activity that requires that a mother step out of her adult world in order to participate in her child's world gives her the opportunity to share in her child's understanding and experiences of his or her world—just as the field-worker who participates in a social function, religious ceremony, or family interaction is given the opportunity to experience another's worldview.

The hermeneutic-type mother uses dialogue to increase her understanding of her child. She explores her child's behavior by asking open, rather than leading, questions; by withholding judgment; by negotiating an understanding. Rather than defining the child's motivations, thoughts, feelings, and actions, she asks the child to define them for her. She might describe to her child what she sees, then ask for an explanation/interpretation. The mother often takes the role of student instead of teacher in her dialogue with the child—she adopts an attitude of curiosity, and an openness to learning about her child's view of the world.

Just as the hermeneutic method involves reflection and reformulation, good mothering involves plenty of self-analysis and a willingness to be flexible and creative in interpreting a child's behavior. We've heard many mothers comment on their tendency to model their own mother's approach to child raising, the recognition of which prompted thoughtful reflection and analysis of which methods to keep and which to reject. The recognition of a separate and subjective reality of individuals (including children) causes the hermeneutic-type mother to examine her own worldview, personal history, and biases, and realize that her child's experiences are as unique and individual as her own. A child's reactions to the world around him or her can often be interpreted only by the one most familiar with the child's history, and then only tentatively—for often the child alone can explain him- or herself with the help and encouragement of carefully constructed questions.

Empathy is a quality inherent in good mothering. The mother has a sense that the child's experience, however limited, is capped by a highest and lowest point just as is her own. In light of this realization, she knows that when her eight-year-old comes home in tears after being rejected by his or her best friend, he or she deserves the same *quality* of empathetic concern as does a grown friend facing a difficult divorce. Likewise, a "student-of-the-month" award deserves the same quality of emotional celebration as a career promotion. An empathetic attitude enables a mother to detect the cause of her child's emotions and validate the experience by sharing the emotion.

In Jean Piaget's theory of child development, he argued that the fundamental nature of thought and reasoning changes with each progressive stage of development. Furthermore, progress from one stage to the next is gradual, evolving from the ongoing interaction with his or her environment. The mother who has invested so many hours "studying" her child and sharing his or her experiences has the raw data to interpret the child's perception of the world. Whether or not she has learned of Piaget's developmental stages, she is aware of her child's reasoning processes and level of intellectual maturation. She is also aware of the process of change from one developmental stage to the next as she witnesses the "discoveries" that lead to her child's progress. The ongoing observation of her child's rational development gives the mother ample opportunity for reflection on and reformulation of her understanding of the child. Hermeneutically speaking, the "text" the mother is studying is definitely not static.

Because of that awareness of her child's cognitive maturity, the mother often becomes an interpreter for her child, explaining his or her behavior, motivations, and reasoning processes from her extensive knowledge based on observation, dialogue, reflection, and reformulation. In a sense, the mother also becomes her child's advocate—interpreting, defending, and empowering her child much as a field-worker might interpret, defend, and empower a culture, subculture, or group that he or she is studying.

It is, perhaps, the recognition of an intersubjective understanding (as opposed to an objective theorizing) that marks the hermeneutic approach to the mother-child relationship. Good mothers *negotiate* an understanding of reality with their children rather than define it in their own terms. In the endeavor to "match horizons," the perceptions and understanding of both mother and child are continually challenged by the ongoing negotiations of understanding—changing, growing, evolving—nourished by the mother through attitudes of humility, curiosity, empathy, and respect.

Exercises

2.1 In dialogical hermeneutic field research, who is responsible for matching horizons? Why? Explain your answer in a short essay.

2.2 Write a short essay to address the following predicament: as an investigator, you get a different picture of an informant's understanding in a second interview.

2.3 In your own words, explain "negotiating truth." What obstacles might prevent an anthropologist from carrying this out?

Note

1. Barry and CherylAnne refer to the authors of the text.

PART II

METHOD

Chapter 3

Design and Sampling

Learning is not attained by chance. It must be sought for with ardor and attended to with diligence.

—Abigail Adams

Before choosing a group to study, we think that it is important to address the question: What constitutes a community or a culture? Modern anthropology continues to wrestle with questions about the nature of ethnicity, culture, and community—the very definitions and usage of these words are at the heart of current debates in the evolution of anthropological thought.

Determining a Community

Current thinking about what constitutes an ethnic group examines the distinction between objective and intersubjective criteria for discerning membership. On the one hand, the investigator determines objective criteria such as the behaviors, traditions, and social structure exhibited by a group or culture. On the other hand, group members choose the intersubjective criteria. They determine the groups to which they are members, and they distinguish fellow group members. We have illustrated these divisions in Figure 3.1.

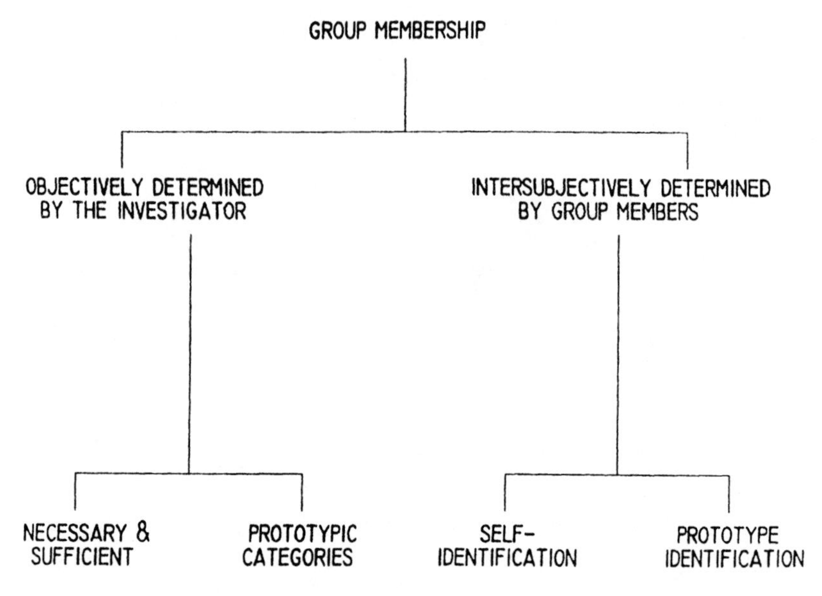

FIGURE 3.1
Method for Determining Group Membership

These two perspectives have two alternatives each. As an investigator you may determine objective measurement by criteria labeled as necessary and sufficient, or by prototypic categories. Some explanation is helpful here. Aristotle originally suggested necessary and sufficient categorization. According to this designation, a group member has a set of features, each of which is necessary and when taken together are sufficient for conferring membership. Thus, a core of traits define membership. If a person has the traits, he or she is "in." If he or she is missing them, the person is "out." An investigator of the group "traditional Navajo" may decide that all traditional Navajo need to speak their native language, attend traditional religious ceremonies, and live on the reservation. By this categorization, those who speak the language and live on the reservation but attend Christian church services rather than traditional religious ceremonies would not be group members.

Using the alternative objective approach, you would look for the widest possible range of features exhibited by group members. Prototype features are not necessarily shared by all the members, but by a substantial number of members, and they are weighted in virtue of how much they are shared. Membership is determined by the extent to which a member embodies the prototype features. This categorization is more "fuzzy edged" than the first. So, for the example of traditional Navajo, additional categories might be added to form the prototype, for example, sheepherder and living close to the wife's relatives. Members do not have to share all features, so a possible informant might include a strict Christian employee of the government because he lives near his wife's relatives, speaks Navajo, and lives on the reservation. Another example of a member of the group based on prototype categories would be a Navajo speaker who teaches school, lives in town near her relatives, and practices the traditional religion.

These would be only two of the many combinations of features which enable you to classify a person as traditional Navajo under the prototype categorization scheme. It is much more flexible than the necessary and sufficient categorization. If you are familiar with set theory in mathematics, you could look at the prototype as a collection of overlapping sets of features. Table 3.1 shows a hypothetical distribution of traits using a prototypic selection of group members.

The intersubjective approach involves the group member's opinion about membership. Does the group member consider him- or herself to be the member of a certain group? This is one intersubjective approach. The other is to ask people who you think qualify as

TABLE 3.1
The Distribution of Traits in the Members Labeled as Navajo by Means of an Objective and Prototypic Measure

	Proportion of the Group with the Trait
1. Language	60%
2. Traditional Religion	35%
3. Native American Church	50%
4. Christian Services	30%
5. Sheepherder	25%
6. Reside on Reservation	50%
7. Has Lived Five or More Years on the Reservation	75%
8. Genetically at Least Fifty Percent Native American	90%
9. Living Close to Wife's Relatives	70%

members of a certain group to designate who they feel are members of their group and why. In either case the insider is choosing the criteria for membership, not the investigator. These may or may not correlate with what others perceive to be objective categories.

Because you will be looking for shared understanding within your chosen community, perhaps the most important aspect to consider is group identity. Would the prospective group members identify *themselves* as a category or community of people? Would the "label" that you would use to describe this group be part of your informants' self-description (i.e., Asian-American, recovering alcoholic, nursing-home resident, etc.). Do the individuals who comprise the group have contact with one another so that they may have the opportunity to share their understanding or worldview—or are they isolated from each other? Do the members have only one characteristic that identifies them or are there many? If only one, is that characteristic "weighty" enough to be considered as an identity? In other words, how life-encompassing is the feature that identifies this group? Consider for example the differences in two groups identified by membership, like Alcoholics Anonymous, whose common goal is sobriety, total life-change, and mutual support; and say, a chapter of the National Rifle Association where you have political activists on one end and armchair "sportsmen" on the other. Take into consideration the bonding aspects of the group you are choosing—support, common life experiences, political interests, language, economics, and employment.

Remember that group members do not have to be in contact with one another to share understandings. For example, prior enculturation may have instilled common values. This was the case for CherylAnne's immigrants from Mexico, some of whom did not know each other, and for Barry's oldest generation of mining families who grew up in a distinctly different era from today within the same geographical area. Many of these people have not known each other.

More questionable are categories of people who have had similar experiences, but who have never been enculturated in a unique culture and who do not communicate. In these cases, it is the experience alone (e.g., living with AIDS or military duty in Vietnam) that defines group members. Do they constitute a subculture? Do they share understandings?

These are all questions to consider—the answers do not necessarily determine which groups are eligible or ineligible for an ethnographic study. However, for a study that is limited in time and area, it would be best to research a group that has (1) a strong sense of identity (identifying *itself* as distinct), (2) intergroup communication, and (3) what you believe to be some shared understanding. Table 3.2 gives some examples of groups considered by students in a qualitative methods class.

Limiting Scope

If you are considering an ethnographic study on the undergraduate level, you are probably looking at one, possibly two, semesters in which to complete your investigation, analyze your information, and write your report. You are facing a fieldwork experience that may also compete for your attention with other course work and/or employment. It is important to consider the logistics involved in fieldwork when designing your study and limiting its scope. You must consider scheduling of interviews that involves the availability and proximity of informants.

In a one-semester course you should expect to conduct ten to twelve lengthy interviews. At least two of these should be follow-up interviews. This means that you should be able to conduct twenty to

TABLE 3.2
Possible Groups to Study

funeral directors	ethnic organizations
Latino neighborhoods	Native American students
a religious school	an African-Am. church
migrant workers	migrant worker services
rodeo club	Loyal Order of the Moose
teen mother program	a nearby historic town
gays	lesbians
the judicial system	the Job Corps Program
a women's book club	a self-help group
a singles club	a divorce support group
coal miners	female miners
welfare families	a high school
administrators	members of a union
an experimental high school	the local welfare admin.
Bikers for Jesus	Seventh Day Adventists
female body-builders	Asian refugees
female exotic dancers	male exotic dancers

thirty interviews in a two-semester course, with four to six follow-up meetings. Should you conduct a summer-long research project you would be interviewing thirty-five to forty times with about eight follow-ups. These numbers will help to guide your consideration of logistics with regard to choice of group and/or informants.

Any group that you choose will contain variability, which you will need to address. It is a good idea to jot down the sources of variability in your proposed group prior to beginning informant selection. For example, the community of Vietnam veterans could include: combat veterans, noncombat, female, male, volunteers, draftees, those with more than one stint, those who had supported the war effort, those who had opposed it, officers and enlisted men/women. What are your options for studying such variability? You should consider eliminating some of the variability or stratifying it for sampling. These are both fairly easy to carry out. By eliminating certain types of informants you limit the scope of your study. So, taking Vietnam veterans as an example, you might reduce informants to male, combat draftees. This still leaves some variability of which you are aware, that is, officer/enlisted, number of stints, and supporter/opposer. Other variability may be exposed during the fieldwork itself.

Any known variability should be used to "stratify" your sample. This term is used in quantitative, statistical studies for which an equal number of respondents/subjects must be chosen from every source of variability. The hermeneutic method is not as rigid in its demands for research design, but it does require that each source of variability have at least one representative. Our rationale for suggesting this is simple: all voices should be heard. It arises from the observation of past mistakes in which one subgroup spoke for the whole group. The other subgroup(s) were not heard. An example involves much of early anthropology in which investigators chose male representatives to speak for the whole culture, leaving the female point of view unspoken.

Since time will be limited in your study, you will want to eliminate some variability as soon as possible. It would make sense for a study involving eight to ten informants to have no more than three or four "voices." Going back to our example of the veterans, at least one informant would have to be chosen from each of the following categories: officer, enlisted man, one stint, more than one stint, supporter, and opposer. All of them would be male combat draftees. We would suggest reducing these categories even further—perhaps to officer, enlisted man, supporter, and opposer. Some of this may need to take place in the field as you get a sense of the availability of informants. The key concept to keep in mind here is that all sources of variability (i.e., voices) that you eliminated or inadvertently missed should be reported in your ethnographic essay. In other words, you should tell your reader in what ways you have limited the study or what voices will not be heard.

SAMPLING

Choosing informants is generally not a random process when doing ethnographic research. This is because of variability in accessibility and quality of informants. It is not always easy to find cooperative informants who have the time to be interviewed, much less the time to develop a trusting relationship with you. Those who you do find may not be insightful enough or articulate enough to give you a meaningful picture of their group. As you may sense from what we are saying here, your finding such an informant will be a rare and important opportunity. For this reason, we say that ethnographic sampling is opportunistic. Your sample does not need to be representative of their group or subgroup in the sense that they have had a "normal" set of experiences. Rather, we see these informants as capable of *representing the understanding* of other group members.

The quality of the interaction and of the information will also help you to determine with whom you will schedule follow-up interviews. Relationships build in this manner.

SUBJECT MATTER

Your study should have a focus of interest—a common theme, issue, problem, celebration, or concern. Many descriptions may lead off from it, but it gives direction and coherence to the study and to the subsequent ethnographic essay. It might help for you to imagine two pictures. In the first are scattered iron filings on a piece of paper. In the second picture a bar magnet under the paper has drawn the filings into a pattern—not crisp and precise, but definitely shaped. A study without focus is like that picture of filings without a magnet. It is scattered. A focused study has a pattern, even if its edges are fuzzy.

We cannot tell you precisely how to choose a focus of interest for your study. In long projects, many topics are likely to surface as you conduct interviews; you have the luxury of waiting for topics to develop. For shorter projects such as the one you will be carrying out, you will need to make a conscious effort to look for leads to follow. For this reason we suggest that you have some theme in mind prior to beginning the study—some question that you want to have answered, some issue that you think might be of importance to your group. Try to be true to yourself about your agenda, making it explicit.

Some examples of such themes are: questions about an afterlife for hospice workers, perceptions of society by juvenile defenders, and motivation for their careers for police officers. With general themes such as these, there is room for the informants to expand the topic to include things that are important to them. You should design a set of open-ended questions to take with you to your interviews, but don't feel obliged to use all of them—or any of them.

Keep in mind that the informants will also have some power to direct the focus. As much as possible give them free rein. One of several scenarios will likely develop, depending on the level of assertiveness of your informants. Passive informants will allow you to maintain the power in choosing the agenda for discussion. They will disclose their agenda in their answers to open-ended questions. More assertive informants will seize the opportunity to transform the interview into an opportunity to express their agenda. Regardless of the level of assertiveness, the informants will be adding irregularity to your original distinct theme. One guideline to keep in mind is that it is proper to guide the informant toward certain issues or themes, but not toward specific opinions about those issues.

Depending on when they develop in your research, you may want to narrow the focus down to one or two side issues. For example, the broad issue of juvenile defenders' view of society might be narrowed to focus on their view of authority figures, of the generation gap, or both.

Another possibility is that your informants (or at least the first few you interview) may totally shift the focus of your study. This would be especially likely when some recent event or policy change has affected the group. Using juvenile defenders as an example, their view of society may be of inconsequential interest to them if their immediate prison environment had recently been altered by the installation of surveillance equipment in their rooms.

As you can see, the design of the study may shift or narrow in focus as the study progresses. In effect, the design is being sculpted over time by the participants; that is, the informants and the investigator. Likewise, the degree of availability of cooperative and articulate informants may have a sculpting influence. For example, your study may shift if good informants cannot be found for any of your modes of variability.

As you may be sensing, a hermeneutic researcher needs to stay flexible, keeping a watchful eye and ear ready to detect where the study will go. The dangers lie in the ethnographer's attitude. If he or she is too rigid the study becomes forced; the information may be redundant or dull. An investigator with such an attitude may feel frustrated through most of the study. On the other extreme, an investigator may be too quick to shift directions, in which case a study may become thin or disjointed. As the ethnographer, you will find that you have to have a certain amount of faith in your original design and a matching faith in the ability to recognize when a plan must shift. Remember to seek guidance on these matters from your instructor and from your support group, should you have one. Also, keep in mind that your field exercise is meant to be a learning process—you may make some design mistakes en route to learning how to gauge how and when to sculpt your study.

Exercises

3.1 Analyze a group that you are fairly serious about studying:
   a. Will group membership be determined by intersubjective or objective criteria?
   b. Will the determination involve prototypes?
   c. If objective, what are the likely criteria?
   d. What will be the connection among members that leads to a shared meaning system?
   e. What voices do you anticipate? Which would you include? Why?

3.2 Write a short essay on the following topic: Some people suggest that objective criteria for group selection has no place in a hermeneutic study. Others suggest that "objective" criteria are really "subjective." How would you address these criticisms?

Chapter 4

Oral Discourse

Without knowing the force of words, it is impossible to know men.

—Confucius

Your goal in your short study will be to try to understand the shared meanings of the group members. Your chief means of gaining discourse for analysis will be the informal interview, though more formal methods may be tried as well. Before we describe these techniques in detail, we want to give you more details of what we mean by shared meaning or shared understanding.

Looking for Shared Understanding

As cultural members, we learn definitions, explanations, values, emotions, and attitudes that our culture attaches to objects, behaviors, rituals, statuses, and relationships. Sometimes we learn these at a very young age and with few words. For example, we may observe our parents' behavior in religious worship and understand without being told that something introspective and meditative is occurring. Children learn their language by being given meaning through discourse. For example, we may be told by parents or teachers that schooling represents the means to a successful and satisfying life. As adults, we may learn the meaning of certain traditions, statuses, and relationships in our specific workplace or profession, in a volunteer organization, in a club or social organization such as the Elks' Club.

Certain subcultures may ascribe different meanings to phenomena that are experienced by many subcultures. In Barry's study of the oldest generation of Pennsylvania coal-mining families, he found that the members of this subculture felt suspicious of the police because they had experienced years of abusive behavior at the hands of the coal and iron police. Most subcultures would not feel such strong resentment and fear at the sight of police officers. CherylAnne, in her study of Mexican immigrant women, found that women had strong feelings about the gender roles specified by that culture.

What you will find as you conduct your study is that your understanding of meaning will not suddenly become clear, distinct, and well-defined. These understandings emerge over time. You might first get a *feeling* of uniqueness in meaning for the people being studied. You may not be able to put this feeling into words until you discuss it further with other informants. As their understanding becomes clearer to you, you may be able to put your view into words, but a concise and explicit description may still be difficult. One reason for this is the holistic nature of many understandings. When the understanding of one relationship, behavior, or object is intertwined with the understanding of several other phenomena, the description becomes more complex.

According to our point of view, oral discourse is the best source of data for understanding the shared meaning of others, and dialogue is the best method. As you learn the shared understanding of others you will be joining their hermeneutic circle. Another way of viewing this is that you will become a member in a community of understanding. You may be limited in your ability to do this in a one semester course, but genuine dialogue with periods of negotiation can be very insightful.

The Hermeneutic Interview

The thought of conducting a loosely structured interview for the first time may strike terror to the heart of many a student fieldworker. To be facing an in-depth conversation with a virtual stranger without the aid of a lengthy survey, a preconceived hypothesis, defined variables, or predictions may seem quite foreign to the student who is schooled in scientific methods; however, with forethought and proper attitudes toward the informant, interviews can be one of the most rewarding aspects of the ethnographic process.

Some attitude adjustments may be required before you attempt to conduct interviews. This attitude must be learned at more than the cognitive (rational and logical) level. You should try to apply your own experiences of indignity, lack of autonomy, exploitation, and arrogance to hone the edge of your empathy for others. We suggest exercises such as 4.1 and 4.2, which are designed to achieve this.

You should review the imperatives of the ethics of hermeneutic interaction—the responsibility to preserve the dignity and autonomy of your informant, and the Kantian ethic: an informant must never be treated merely as a means to an end. You must also reflect on the issue of power, adjusting your attitude from the "one-up" position of researcher addressing subject to the "one-down" position of a student addressing a teacher.

Your informant may have some preconceived ideas/expectations about the nature of the interview. Chances are, he or she has never been questioned by a student with a hermeneutic perspective and does not know what to expect. Your initial task is to give an adequate explanation of your study; its scope, its intent, its goals, and the methods by which you reach your conclusions. Although it is not necessary to present a minicourse in hermeneutics, we feel that it is important to attempt an explanation of your purpose and your process in order to set the stage for meaningful dialogue.

In CherylAnne's study of Mexican immigrant women, she began each interview with a new informant in this manner, keeping her explanation as simple as possible because of the difficulty in dealing with two languages. Basically, she told her informants that her study was not a scientific study that sought to *explain* their group to the larger population. Rather, that it was a study based on dialogue (conversation) from which she sought to gain an understanding of their lives, attitudes, and culture with the intent of adequately *describing* them to her readers. She emphasized the idea of a better understanding, pointing out that she hoped to dispel some of the stereotypes commonly held and replace them with the informants' view of who they are as individuals and as a community of people.

At the beginning of each interview, she attempted to break the ice with casual conversation, finding it easy to ask about her informant's children, or about some culinary delight that was simmering on the kitchen stove. She found that by conversing on common ground for the first few minutes, she established herself as a peer, removing or diminishing any intimidation that her informant might have been experiencing. Laughter, in those initial minutes, was also a great tension reliever, and with her faulty Spanish, there was ample occasion for it. So try not to take yourself *too* seriously, and remember that humor, when appropriate, can defuse a tense situation.

You should prepare some questions for each interview. You may not use all of the questions, but they are often a starting point. We have found that whenever we start with a prepared question, our informant's response would generate new questions. Sometimes new questions would be necessary to clarify or elaborate on a specific response; at other times, the response would lead naturally into other, related areas. We try to allow the conversation to flow without attempting to maintain control of its direction because we feel that it is important to allow informants the freedom to talk about what *they* perceive as important. When we have exhausted a particular line of thought, we will move to another prepared question.

You should formulate open-ended questions that stimulate the informant to give you more than a yes/no answer. Table 4.1 gives a list of closed questions followed by similar questions written in an open-ended fashion. As you can see, closed questions can be answered with a simple "yes" or "no." It is fine to include a few closed questions; however, the majority should be open-ended.

You will encounter many different personalities in your interviews. Some informants will be open and eager to share; others will be more guarded. We have found it difficult, initially, to gain the trust of certain informants, even after describing the study, methods, and ethics regarding ethnography. There may be any number of sensitive issues involved in your discourse with a member of the group you have chosen to study. We found that our informants better understood *our* purpose, and became more open with us when we made ourselves vulnerable to *them*. Self-disclosure invites self-disclosure, and when we prefaced a question by telling our informants about our own personal experience, or our own preconceived notions about their culture, we were displaying our trust by being transparent. The interaction felt like we were "laying all of our cards on the table" and inviting them to do the same—without pressure or a

TABLE 4.1
Converting Closed Questions to Open-Ended

Closed Questions:

1. Do you think you will get a job in your field when you graduate?
2. Are you satisfied with the courses in your major?
3. Do you think that the curriculum could be improved?
4. Do you know any people who graduated in your field?
5. How many courses did you have to take in your major?
6. Would you recommend this field of study to others?
7. Is employment in your field growing?

Open-ended Questions:

1a. What do you see as some of the job possibilities for you when you graduate?
1b. What are your feelings about job prospects when you graduate?
2. How would you assess the courses in your major?
3a. In what ways do you think that the curriculum could be improved?
3b. What are your impressions of the curriculum?
4. What are some of the graduates in your field like?
5. What sort of course work was required for your major?
6. What would you say to people considering this field of study?
7. In what ways do you perceive the job prospects to be changing?

sense of prying. Often we would preface a question by saying, "It has been my experience where I grew up that . . . ; how do you, personally or as a culture, view this same thing?" or "I've observed among your group that . . . ; I'm not sure I understand; can you explain this to me?"

In this same vein are reflective questions or reflective statements. We use these to paraphrase and reflect back what the informant has told us. Since these indicate an empathy with one's informants, they are referred to by some people as empathic response leads. They give the informant the impression that you really are listening, and they help to ensure that you have properly understood the gist of what they are saying. Table 4.2 lists some empathic response leads. We suggest that you memorize two or three and practice using them in everyday conversation. Then you will use them naturally in your interviews.

It is very important that you phrase questions in a way that does not lead your informant or presuppose a certain answer. Never

TABLE 4.2
Empathetic Response Leads

As I understand it, you felt that . . .
I'm picking up that you . . .
If I'm hearing you correctly . . .
To me it's almost like you are saying, "I . . ."
So, what you feel is . . .
What I hear you saying is . . .
So, as you see it . . .
I really hear you saying that . . .
You appear to be feeling . . .
So, from where you sit . . .
You must have felt . . .

ask if something is "this way or that way?"—What if your informant's answer does not fit into either category that you have set before him or her? Also, try to avoid "loaded language," that is, words with highly connotative meanings that reveal your own feelings and have the potential of stifling your informant's freedom of response. For example, asking "How would John and his henchmen run the organization?" obviously relays the message that you perceive of John's cohorts as wrongdoers. Referring to them as "cohorts" or as "assistants" would not trap the informant into inadvertently agreeing with you or going out of his or her way to disagree with you.

If you maintain an open mind, continually reflect on and attempt to identify your personal biases, and keep the humble attitude of student, you will develop a sensitivity to leading and "loaded" questions and avoid them. The avoidance of leading questions displays respect toward your informant—his or her autonomy of expression—as well as leads to more reliable data.

Many students find a tape recorder useful in interviews; however, there are a few things to consider before opting to use recording equipment. The very presence of a tape recorder is intimidating to some people and can have a stifling effect on the informant. In our society, tapes are so often associated with surveillance, espionage, and media or legal interrogations that it may be difficult to shake the negative feelings associated with them. Also, it is extremely painstaking and time consuming to transpose, word-for-word, the contents of a single hour of conversation. Many students find that a note pad and pencil are the most practical tools to use in the interview. It may be worthwhile to develop your own personal "shorthand" in order to be able to fully catch your informants' responses—not only the content, but the color of their unique expression. We have found that when we made notes during the interviews, coupled with some exact quotes from informants, we were able to write out the interview from memory *if* we set about the task immediately afterward. By keeping our notes brief during the interview, we found that we could maintain eye contact with informants, and also stay aware of facial expressions, gestures, and posture that often gave us additional information. It is important to stress that your notes must be transcribed into your field journal as soon as possible following an interview. Memory fades quickly, and much of your information will be lost or distorted if you allow time to pass between the actual interview and its transcription.

If you keep in mind that your interviews are a negotiation process in which your goal is to share another's understanding of their world, you should not find it difficult to incorporate the attitudes that encourage responsiveness in your informant. Your own open-mindedness, curiosity, and humility (that "one-down" position) are the attitudes that both display and invite trust and openness. Mutual respect between field-worker and informant is the natural byproduct of these attitudes, and an essential ingredient to the understanding of another.

Formal Methods

Some students may feel that they are pressed for time or that they need to give their study coherence or focus. This is especially likely in a project that is limited to the duration of one semester. In this case you may want to formalize your interviewing techniques—giving them more structure and focus. We have tried, or have been informed of, the following formalized methods: training courses, preference questioning, if-then questioning, photograph interpretation, psychological games and term categorization.

Some students have chosen groups that require specialized instruction. Examples include: AIDS advocacy volunteers, hospice volunteers, and Loyal Order of the Moose membership. Formalized instruction in all these cases involved written material as well as oral instruction. The philosophy of the organization was expressed in addition to rules and methods of behavior. In cases such as these the discourse provided by the trainers can be data for understanding the group. It is also a source of information for future dialogues with group members.

Preference questions ask the informant to choose the preferred condition in a list of two or more or to rank their preferred conditions from best to worst. The answers themselves may be tabulated, but of greater interest will be the conversations catalyzed by this process. Informants will tell you why they made their choices, why selection was difficult, or why they prefer to not answer certain questions. The formality of the question does not lead to more formal data so much as to more insightful and focused responses. An example might be to ask them whether they prefer to work for the government, for big business, for a small business, or for a nonprofit organization.

A second type of formalized question is the if-then question. It is a technique to expand your current understanding of the culture and a way to foment challenges to your description. It is a way to have informants react to assumptions being made about them by the news media, by government studies, or by you as the investigator. For example, you might ask: "If the newspapers are right in describing your union as radical in its orientation, then how do you think you would go about getting support from the general public?" Other aspects to this question could be: ". . . then why did you reject other possibilities? . . . then who was the leader for this point of view? . . . then what are future plans based on that orientation?"

In the case of both the preference and the if-then questions, you need to carry out some research to give you a basis for designing the questions. This research could include initial interviewing; analysis of fictional accounts of these people; and analysis of prior research by others.

Barry found in his study of the oldest generation of coal miners and their wives that photographs lent to him by some informants worked well as a catalyst for insightful discussion. While not feasible for all studies, this method enables the investigator to ask for interpretation of the events in the photos or identification of those people and places pictured.

A student doing a study of teenage boys in a detention center recommended a method of asking informants to fill out a questionnaire that could be constructed from the type of questions common to psychological parlor games. She found her informants to be very cooperative, in part due to the fact that she also filled out the questionnaire for their examination. Some example questions include: "What is your definition of success? One thing I missed in my childhood was ______ . What do you think about when you can't sleep?" The answers to the questionnaire provide data; however, what you may find more helpful is the opportunity for extensive conversations as a result of the method.

Term categorization is a method derived from cognitive anthropology. Ethnographers such as Catherine Lutz and Michael Agar have used this method in their analyses. It works best for cultures with a language other than English or with a heavy use of slang terms.

Lutz used this technique to examine the cognitive organization of emotion categories on the island of Ifaluk. She recognized thirty-one emotion words in the Ifaluk language that she used for a card sort among thirteen informants. She then analyzed the groupings for structure, finding that the categorization was based on the situation in which the relevant emotion typically occurs.

Agar used it to understand the worldview of drug users. He interviewed drug patients at a Lexington, Kentucky, hospital and junkies on the street. He placed junkie slang on cards and asked sorters to place cards into the same piles if they were different ways of saying the same thing.

Other subcultures might include professions or work occupations that have a unique terminology. In order to use this technique you will first have to compile a list of terms or phrases commonly used within the group you are studying. We know of three methods for compiling such a list: listening sessions, analysis of written material, or frame elicitation.

Your listening sessions could take place where your informants gather. Barry heard conversations among retired coal miners in bars and at union meetings. CherylAnne participated in church services that were frequented by some of her informants. You will want to listen for slang expressions, common expressions used in unique situations or to describe unique situations, and for expressions with higher than usual frequency of use.

Another source of terms and phrases might be literature in which your group members are described or quoted, archival sources such as newspaper articles, letters to the editor and personal letters. The most obtrusive method is frame elicitation. In this case the anthropologist writes a series of short paragraphs in which the last line contains a blank to be filled in by informants. This is a way to get the group members' terms for those situations, events, interactions, and behaviors that you have noticed to be common and/or important to them. This works best with foreign languages, but could work for slang terms if used in conjunction with the analysis of listening sessions and of written material. Sometimes a phrase rather than a term may be used in a uniquely descriptive fashion.

Once you make the list of terms and phrases, you will need to transfer it to a series of small cards—one term (or phrase) per card. You will ask informants to sort terms into piles based either on their similarity or on their relatedness. You may want to include standard English terms in your pile of cards. Cognitive anthropologists have several complicated procedures that they use to analyze the results of the sorting. We suggest that dialogical information obtained as a result of the sorting is more important. You should ask informants whether they perceive any ambiguity in performing the sorting, and then inquire into its nature. You could also inquire into the differences in sorting by each informant—Why do they occur? Finally, you might ask each informant about the nature of the categories that they chose. Catalyzing the elicitation of focused dialogue is the chief benefit of this and all the formal methods described here.

Unfortunately, there can be a price to pay for such formality. One shortcoming is the power differential created with these methods. You, as investigator, will have the power to control the conversation—there is much less give-and-take. Besides dealing with the ethics involved in such a power difference, you may also find that many informants elect to decline participation in the exercise. Another shortcoming involves trust. A request made to participate in exercises that the informant does not understand may feel threatening to some informants, and this may jeopardize your potential relationships with them. Conduct these methods with these risks in mind.

We hope that these instructions on the methods of discourse to understand shared meanings of your group will give you some sense of where to start and how to proceed in your interactions with your group. Try not to be overly concerned with what is "right" or "best." Much of fieldwork is intuitive, and none of us is perfect.

Read this chapter thoroughly, outline it, and then put the book and outline aside for awhile. At this point you will be ready to "jump into the field" and follow your common sense. Often we learn much from our initial mistakes, so you will likely benefit from your early encounters, regardless of their nature.

EXERCISES

4.1 Carry out this procedure in groups of two:
  a. Interview each other with a list of five questions, sticking strictly to the questions;
  b. Reinterview in a more loose manner, using reflective questions and rephrasing. Try to get a natural dialogue flowing. Do not worry if you do not get past question 1;
  c. Write an essay describing the difference in the processes for you and the differences in the data collected.

4.2 In groups of two or three, talk about your own experiences with arrogant people, with times in which you felt a lack of respect, and of times when you felt used by others.

4.3 In groups of two, role play a situation in which one of you plays the part of a naive and cooperative person and the other plays the part of an arrogant and exploitive person. Scenarios could include a clerk and customer pair, a student and professor pair, and a policeman and suspect pair. Switch roles and try again. How did it feel to be arrogant and exploitive? How did it feel to be mistreated?

4.4 As best you can, explain conscious reasons for choosing your topic and group for study. Also, identify any possible unconscious reasons that you *might* have (e.g., studying train tramps because you have had an unconscious desire to be free of all responsibilities). In reflecting, you want to make the unconscious into something conscious and able to be articulated.

4.5 a. Identify a topic or issue to be explored in the study of your group.
  b. Design ten open-ended questions for your informants.
  c. Reassess the boundaries of your group, that is, the number of voices that you wish to include. Also, reconsider the setting(s) in which you plan to find your informants.

Chapter 5

Field Notes and Journals

We begin to know one another most through the doubts, awkward greetings, and frail truths owned by any conversation.

—Robert R. Desjarlais

Field Notes

Field notes constitute the heart of the ethnographic method, yet the process of keeping a field notebook is difficult to describe. Virtually everything you describe in your ethnography will come from either the field notes or the reflective journal. Thus, you will need to record the context of your interactions and interviews as well as descriptions of behaviors (particularly for textual hermeneutics) and dialogues.

It is easy to become overwhelmed by the wealth of notable context when first beginning the investigation. We anthropologists call this "first entering the field." We liken it to the effect on a beginning art student of being introduced to the concepts of "design" and "negative space" and then being sent out to look for it. It is virtually everywhere. The novice's eyes are filled with this data. He or she is no longer looking at the world in a concrete fashion. The brain of the novice becomes overloaded with the myriad design elements in both positive and negative space. So it is with the novice field worker. Your mind will become overloaded with the myriad pieces of information flooding in on you from the reality being experienced. The importance of note-taking will intensify your awareness; everything will appear new and important. It will be likely that you will become discouraged soon after entering the field because early note-taking is so demanding and so unfocused. With persistence and patience, you will reach a point where you can be more selective in your note-taking. By writing a research proposal prior to entering the field, you can avoid some of the adjustment, even though your research interest is likely to change, especially with long-term research.

If you take notes at the time of observation or interview, you should use some type of shorthand. By practicing its use for at least two weeks, you will find yourself employing it automatically. Some investigators drop vowels in the words they write, some just write the first few letters of words, some create abbreviations for commonly used words such as "rxn" for reaction. It is important to review the field notes as soon as possible following the entry so that you can identify the words being represented.

The same rule holds true for those cases in which you are unable to take notes at the time of observation or conversation. The longer the delay, the more likely you are to put your own interpretation into the notes.

It is best to make entries in a bound "composition book" rather than in a book from which pages may easily be torn. We have found that pages may be regrettably torn from our field notes—anything entered may eventually prove important. Entries need not be made directly on receiving the data. At times we have entered notes directly during conversations, but at other times we have also taken notes in a notebook such as a steno pad and have transferred them to the field notebook immediately following the interview. The advantages of transferring the information include improved legibility, addition of details from memory, and the change from shorthand to regular spelling.

It is important to distinguish quotations according to the accuracy in which you have recorded them. We recommend placing double quotations around statements that you feel certain are direct, single quotation marks around statements that are likely those expressed but that require some use of your memory, and no quotation marks in the case of paraphrasing. When you write a report from an analysis of your notes you will be glad that you have some sense of the accuracy of informant quotations.

We suggest making entries on only one side of the page. This leaves the facing page available for additional observations or analyses. You may want to record the context of an interview on the facing page. For example, you could record the place and time of the interview, the duration of the interview, any interruptions or other breaks in frame, facial expressions, or hand movements. The facing page can also be used to record your questions to the informants while the replies are recorded on the major page. When recording by hand (not taped), you may sometimes find yourself skipping the process of writing down what you say or ask. You can compensate by adding these later from memory. The following is an example of this notebook technique.

ME: Like a cultural "support system?", a common ground situation?

H.G.: Yes. We have something in common right off.

NOTE: Get back to this! Next visit ask what is this shared culture?
values?
worldview?

V.M.: It's like that for me—at a conference or anywhere like that—you look for other Hispanics. Also, I feel a great pride when a Hispanic gets up and makes a good speech or receives an award. Like that person is one of us—there's a strong identification. You wouldn't feel that way would you, at a speech or something like that?

ME: You mean if an Anglo person were up there? No, I don't feel that kind of identification with that person. Except in the case of a woman, one that maybe has struggled against the odds to achieve what she has.

V.M.: Yes. I feel that way when it's a woman, too. That's one of the first things I tell women from Mexico. I say, "You're not in Mexico anymore—you have rights here."

You might also begin analyses on the facing pages. As you collect data you should begin constructing descriptions or understandings of various situations. In the same way that we found initial data collection to be somewhat overwhelming, we found initial analyses to be abundant. During early fieldwork you may feel like a pinball bouncing from insight to insight. Often these initial insights are based on rather scant data and do not hold up following further data collection; however, this is a useful process that should be pursued. The following insights come from Barry's field notes:

> Thoughts concerning local bars:
>
> 1. For males they seem to provide for a solidarity across the generations. Ages from twenty-one to over seventy are usually represented—and they interact. Often fathers and sons will be in the same bar.
>
> 2. By excluding females they seem to exempt them from important social ties and from having a "place to go." I'm sure that patrons and owners alike would deny any overt exclusion (except for private male clubs), but I think that they would be dissatisfied with 50 percent female attendance. It seems that females feel a yearning to get out of the area at a young age because there is nothing to do and because it is so difficult to meet a prospective mate.

You will find it helpful to begin indexing your entries on a regular basis (perhaps every ten to twenty pages). This requires that you note regularities in people's choice of topics or replies to certain questions. By designating a symbol for each subject (for example a star for discourse about death or a triangle for discourse about luck) and placing the symbol in the margin of the entry, you provide yourself with a way to quickly locate subjects throughout your notes. This will become valuable both for your continuing descriptions and for your writing phase. Be certain to include a key in the front of your field notebook in which you identify each symbol. We give an example of such a key in chapter 7.

Maintaining the privacy of individuals is crucial, so you need to code the names of your informants. Some investigators have used names such as Greek gods and goddesses; others have used a system of numbers and letters. The key for the identification of persons by code should be kept separate from the field notes. An example of a code might involve the first letter of the first name along with a number or letter for sex, age, class, occupation, and so on. So, a 1 or 2 could be used for male or female; C,A,Y,M, or E could code for child, adolescent, young adult, middle-aged, and elder; U,M,W, or P could code for upper, middle, working, and poor class; and 0,1,2,3, or

4 could code for unemployed, clerical, maintenance, supervisory, and professional occupations. Thus, someone could be identified as C1MP2 (Charles, a middle-aged, male, maintenance worker of the poorest class).

THE REFLECTIVE JOURNAL

Writing a reflective journal seems to come easily to some students, while others have a difficult time recording anything that is not based on concrete data. Reflective journal entries should include such things as thoughts, feelings, presuppositions, and personal history. These may seem to some students to be more like psychological therapy than ethnography; however, reflection is essential to the hermeneutic method, for it is through reflection that the investigator discovers personal biases, projections, and transferences, and becomes aware of "challenges."

If the goal in a hermeneutic study is that the investigator and subjects come to an understanding, or "match horizons," it is necessary for you, the investigator, to come to a conscious awareness of just what "horizon" or worldview you are bringing to the study. It has been our experience that, in asking our informants questions about their worldview, we not only prompted them to think about *their* culture, but we were compelled to answer the very questions we posed to them for ourselves. For example: in CherylAnne's study of Mexican immigrants, she asked her informants questions about their sense of identity as a people. In her reflective journal, she wrestled with this very question herself, trying to discover her own worldview, specifically, whether or not she had a sense of belonging to her culture. In attempting to answer for herself the same questions she asked her informants, she not only realized the degree of difficulty inherent in some of her queries, but also the preconceived structure through which she would tend to interpret their answers. This latter aspect helped her to recognize assumptions she might be making, and to formulate new questions required to gain an unbiased understanding.

Reflection also provides the instrument necessary to detect transference. Transference takes place when the investigator relates to his or her informant in a way that mimics another interpersonal relationship in his or her life. In a journal, you have the opportunity to note personal feelings about the interaction between yourself and the informant. You might address the question: "How do I feel about this informant? How do I feel about what he or she is telling me?" Barry made such a journal entry in January, 1988:

> When SHL182 asked me questions about how I earned my living and when I was going to look for permanent employment, I felt as if he might be nagging me about getting a decent job. Since he is old enough to be a parent or grandparent, I was likely having a transference of parental interaction, which likely distorted the nature of his questioning.

If the informant presents a strong resemblance to someone you know or have known in the past—either in the content of his or her dialogue, or in mannerisms displayed—you must examine yourself for transference. Sometimes, simply the status of the informant will trigger a transference: that is, an investigator who had a poor relationship with his or her father might transfer elements of that relationship to the interaction with the informant simply because the informant happens to be a father. In some studies, such as those of Abraham Rosman, Catherine Lutz, or Jean Briggs, the investigators were adopted by informants. In these cases the likelihood of transference would increase greatly. As the native "parents" play their roles, the investigator may begin to feel like a child and react toward them as he or she would as a teenager with natural parents. For example, Jean Briggs's overly protective and controlling Utku "father" may have caused her to react in angry rebellion. One interpretation of her feelings and acts is that she experienced a negative transference. We include further information about transference, including other examples, in chapter 7. If you feel that you need further clarification at this point, you may wish to look at it now.

Projections may also become evident through journal entries. Projection occurs when the investigator attributes his or her own thoughts, feelings, or emotions to the informant. For example, you might interpret a facial expression, a tone of voice, or certain words as being indicative of anger because you are angry about the issue that your informant is describing. CherylAnne wrote the following entry in her journal:

> . . . Sometimes during the winter, I would go one or two weeks without seeing anyone but my husband and children. My role

> was well defined and I was committed to it, but I *was* lonely. I have to watch out that I am not *projecting* my feelings from those years onto Carla's situation.

Social, political, or interpersonal relationships about which you have strong feelings *will* color the data received from your informants. Reflection through journal writing will enable you to identify those strong feelings and preconceptions, and thereby determine whether or not you are "leading" your informants toward information that fits into preconceived notions or structures, or misinterpreting what they say. For example, in CherylAnne's study, she came to an awareness of her own strong feelings about male dominance in Anglo society through what she wrote in her reflective journal. With this realization, she was able to carefully construct her questions (and later her analysis) about "machismo" and traditional Hispanic male/female roles so that her own bias did not influence her informants' responses or her interpretation of those responses.

It is important to note here that investigator bias—always viewed as a detriment to scientific study—can be used to a positive end in a hermeneutic study. When personal bias is confronted and analyzed in your reflective journal, it can lead to increased sensitivity toward your informants. Furthermore, when your bias is divulged to the reader of the ethnographic work, the reader is given the opportunity to observe the effort you took to identify and control the effect of your bias on the study, and can determine for him- or herself what effect that bias had on your conclusions.

Feelings about how the study is going are also important to record. You can use these during the writing phase to place yourself within the study, illustrating to readers the frustration of fieldwork. The following is an example from Barry's journal:

> Recent trips to the Inn and to the Tavern have been not only unproductive, but anxiety-provoking. Sitting alone at a bar with scant recognition from the bartender for hours at a time, while people are grouped together, some of whom I know, gives me the fear of never fitting in and thus of having an unsuccessful field experience.

At the beginning of your study, you will use the reflective journal to examine your thoughts and feelings about the group you have chosen to study. You may want to begin by addressing these questions:

1. Why have I chosen this community of people?
2. How do I feel about them (sympathetic, superior, intimidated, anxious, etc.)?
3. What are my preconceived notions about this community?
4. Where do these notions come from?
5. What do I think I will find out in this study?

After the fieldwork has begun, the interviews and observations will become the main source of stimulus for reflection. You may want to answer the very questions you used in your interviews to discover your own attitudes or worldview. However, spontaneous thoughts or conversations that occur outside of the context of the study may paint a more accurate picture of your true value system. Cultivating the reflective journal "habit" will increase your awareness of your own thoughts, words, feelings, and actions.

When you are in the midst of ethnographic fieldwork, the study somehow permeates every aspect of your life—personal relationships, other courses of study, self-discovery—all seem to be affected by your research. For this reason, it may be helpful to pay special attention to your dreams during this time. A dream may offer a significant metaphor or picture that identifies a "challenge" or pricks your conscience with an ethical concern. Some people find it useful to jot down in a few phrases the subject of a dream so that they can recall it in the morning. You might want to keep a notepad and pencil on the nightstand for this purpose. The following is an example of a dream entry from Barry's journal:

> *Dream #1:* I ride downstream in a boat and get out in a town and write this message on a blackboard at the dock: "There is no such thing as a free ride."
>
> *Dream #2:* I approach the back of CAA134's house. She comes out and looks haggard. I say to her that she doesn't look well, and I touch her arm. From the open door the town grocer asks, "Are you going to be there tonight?" CAA134 resolutely goes back in and sits back down to talk with two other people.
>
> *Interpretation:* I have a debt (responsibility) to my other informants and need to meet those obligations rather than taking the free ride down the stream of talking to new people every night.

While introspection and a "stream-of-consciousness" approach to journal writing can produce useful material for your study, it is important to keep in mind the purpose and function of the reflective journal in hermeneutic ethnography. The reflective journal is not the place to document your own personal journey toward self-actualization; it is the place to document the *process* of your fieldwork in all of the aforementioned aspects. Your personal introspection should *relate* to your study; it should "connect" with a discovery you have made about the community you have chosen to describe.

During the semester that CherylAnne conducted her fieldwork, she found herself making connections between what she was learning about the community of people she was studying and the other activities in her life. A conversation with a friend, a lecture in another class, a piece of literature or music, a random thought, would "connect" with some aspect of fieldwork experience, providing a fresh insight, metaphor, or new question. By seizing these connections and committing them to her reflective journal, she was able to document the process of ethnography—the gradual unfolding of an increasing understanding. All such "connections" have a place in the reflective journal even if they seem trivial at the time. Much of what may seem to be rambling or philosophizing may not become a part of the final ethnographic work; however, those reflective "mental flights" may contain that gem of insight that becomes the tying theme to your entire study. You should feel a freedom of expression in the reflective journal that allows you to explore and speculate without criticism.

Although field notes must be completed as soon as possible following each interview, the reflective journal documents the ongoing process of the study; therefore, entries can be made at any time. However, it is important to reflect on each interview while it is fresh in your mind. Besides reflecting for possible transferences or projections, you need to examine your informant's responses to determine if he or she has presented you with any "challenges" to your present understanding. Ask yourself if you find any of the responses confusing or ambiguous. If so, what might you ask in a follow-up interview that might clarify your understanding? What new information has come to light? What information supports what you have been told by others?

The reflective journal is as important to the hermeneutic method of research as the interviews and field notes. If reflection does not come naturally to you, it is important to make the effort to cultivate it. A study rich in reflection will result in an ethnography rich in understanding and insight.

EXERCISES

5.1 Rutherford A. Doright, a male anthropology student (age 23) was conducting fieldwork in an Arizona mining community. He found a fifty-four-year-old widow, Rosa, from whom he could rent a room and have meals. Because she had many connections in the community, she facilitated his sampling. After having lived on cafeteria food for four years, he was glad to have home-cooked meals, served in a caring way. He and Rosa would talk during the meals, and she would often ask him questions about how his study was going—what he was learning. He preferred to not talk about it, but he didn't tell her so.

One day while eating supper she asked him about his interview with Pepe, a young miner. Rutherford told her that while Pepe did not say so, he seemed to resent his wife asking questions every day about what went on in the mine. Rosa replied, "Oh, I don't think so. Pepe and Maria are such a loving couple, always sharing. I think that you might be misunderstanding him." Rutherford felt his pulse quickening; he was suddenly uncontrollably angry. He threw his napkin onto his plate and shouted, "All you ever do is pry into my life—then you don't believe what I tell you anyhow. I'm sick of it!" He got up from the table and stomped to his room. After a half hour of stewing about the situation, Rutherford cooled down and fell asleep. He dreamed that a huge shark was chasing him through the water and that it found him everywhere he hid. He finally was cornered against a pile of rocks. As he faced his doom the shark changed into a puppy, and Rutherford and he were sitting in the sun on a warm spring day. When he awoke, he reflected on the day's events. He made a lengthy entry in his reflective journal before going out in the kitchen to apologize to Rosa.

Speculate on what Rutherford wrote in his journal, assuming that he is good at self-analysis. Could a challenge be involved in any way? Write your answer in the form of a short essay.

5.2 Group into pairs. One member should interview the other on an agreed on topic, and after five or ten minutes give a short description of the views of the "informant"—the anthropologist's interpretation of the other. Did the "informant" find the description to be accurate?

5.3 Group into pairs. Have one member formulate ten or so questions on a specific topic and present them to the second student a day before class so that he or she is able to write replies. On the class day conduct the interview with the "informant" reading answers. The "investigator" should try to write from memory the questions and answers from the interview. Both participants check the accuracy of the remembered interview with the written preinterview. What did this teach you about memory and interviewing?

Chapter 6

The Personal and the Interpersonal

I have met few ethnographers who were not personally affected in some profound way by their fieldwork.

—Michael H. Agar

Fieldwork using the dialogical hermeneutic method is largely an experience of personal feelings and interpersonal interactions. You will likely face many self-doubts, fears, self-recriminations, old ghosts, and new challenges. Informants may bring you joy, sadness, shame, frustration, grief, guilt, and anger. This is why a personal journal is so important—partly as a catharsis, partly to get in mind *how* you feel exactly, and partly to console yourself and make new plans.

Emotional Support

For most students this writing is not enough to help them through the process. A support group with whom you can share issues of a personal and interpersonal nature is tremendously helpful. But where do you find such a group? While friends and family may help somewhat, these groups are limited in two ways: (1) they are not doing fieldwork, so they may have a difficult time understanding and empathizing with your emotional highs and lows, and (2) they may have a difficult time maintaining the confidentiality you will need for your informants.

Your classmates who are also doing fieldwork will make a uniquely supportive group. They will be able to relate to many of the emotion-laden experiences that you may need to tell. Sometimes knowing that someone else is having an experience similar to yours is reassuring—or that they have made it through such an experience. They may be able to offer suggestions based on experience or be gently encouraging. They will be relating their trials, failures, and successes, letting you know indirectly that you are not alone. It would be best if a person with good group-leading skills conducted regular sessions with six to fifteen students. Your instructor or a mature teaching assistant would be ideal. The officialness of the meeting (replacing one class period a week?), its regularity, its structured leadership, and its confidentiality will give you the sense of a safety net from which you can count on feedback and support.

We do not mean to frighten you with this talk about emotions and the need for support. The fieldwork situation is one in which you will be taking risks to create new situations and new relationships with total strangers, and the success of your project depends on these contacts. Some topics of conversation that we can relate from support group interaction include: entering a gay bar for the first time; being told again and again that you are not allowed to have access to the informants who you have located; being told by a key informant that he or she is lying; being told by a key informant that he or she wants his or her conversation deleted; dealing with many incoherent, self-absorbed informants (e.g., elderly residents of a nursing home); being in a situation in which everyone but the student has a gun; being insulted by an informant; being "stood up" by an informant; finding that your intended group does not really exist; witnessing the mistreatment of your informants; finding that you cannot focus your study; or being entrusted with information you would rather have not heard.

You may find that during the course of a semester of such group meetings that you form close ties with group members. Openness builds trust quickly. These interpersonal relations will have emotions associated with them as well—although you mostly have warm feelings, you may at times feel slighted, betrayed, insulted, or ignored by group members.

Getting Started

So, with your journal and your support group as allies, and with your copy of Michrina and Richards as a guide, you are ready to face the personal and interpersonal in your project. This is likely to start with being too anxious to start.

Whether it is due to excitement, fear of failure, or fear of rejection, most people have a difficult time getting started in fieldwork. Making the first contact is difficult. It means putting yourself on the line to try to get fruitful cooperation. One message that you might repeat to yourself during the beginning phase (and perhaps throughout the study) is that anything you try will bring you data. Since you are keeping a journal, any rejection, any awkward interaction, any embarrassment will be data for the journal. This may end up in your final report as self-critique, as characteristics of the group (e.g., perhaps gays will not cooperate with you because you are a straight male), or as amusing anecdote. Jean Paul Dumont and David Borshay Lee, among others, have included self-deprecating anecdotes in their writings. Both described their being ridiculed for their naivete about the ways of their informants. Dumont also described his maladroit attempts at hunting and his embarrassment in dressing like the Amazon natives. Laughing at one's self eases one's anxiety and amuses the reader.

So, pick up that phone or knock on that first door. Say your line that you have memorized, then start taking data—you have begun. It will be as easy as that.

Early in your research you will hope to find two types of cooperative people—those who are knowledgeable and articulate and those who can help you make contacts within your group of study. The latter can be of great help in lubricating your social relations. He or she might "put in a good word for you," or tell you to "tell them I said that you should talk to her," or actually introduce you to the others. This is such a valuable service that you might consider asking for one of these favors if it is not offered spontaneously. Make sure that you let your "facilitator" know exactly what kind of information you are looking for: for example, historical, official policy, life experiences, critical analysis, or first impressions. Do you want someone who is a supervisor or someone with experience "in the trenches"?

Those people who give you your most valuable information are called key informants. These will be the people who you choose for follow-up interviews. Perhaps you will interview them even more often or build a lasting relationship with them. What qualities give rise to people becoming key informants? They are usually people who have a deep knowledge of the subject matter and a way of expressing this knowledge that is very understandable. The understanding that they transfer might come from the logical fashion in which they lay out the information or might be the result of the colorful language they employ, rich in metaphors and emotion. The sadness, joy, solemnity, or anger will come across in the words of the account. Usually, enthusiasm is a vital quality as well. These people live their account—this is something they need or want to say. They will want you to meet with them again, and they will view you and your project in positive terms.

Knowledge of the subject is not enough. When Barry did his study of retired coal miners and their wives, he received recommendations to go and talk to certain men because of their technical knowledge about mining. Most of these leads were disappointing because the informants lacked the understanding of the human side of the occupation—of relationships and emotions.

Incidentally, you should not take personally any difficulty you have in setting up an appointment with someone. We have often left a series of messages on an answering machine that go unanswered; we have had potential informants reply in a vague manner about setting an appointment to talk; and we have been "stood up" by potential informants. It was easy to imagine that such people were avoiding us, but in most instances important issues in their lives were interfering with their willingness to cooperate with us. Our experiences suggest that in most cases your patience and persistence in setting up interviews will be rewarded.

Fieldwork Relationships

Because you will have such good rapport with your field facilitator and key informants, you will likely develop a friendship with them. This will be more likely the longer your study. A trust builds quickly if you are open about your feelings—especially your fears. The informant then feels free to express his or her emotions as well. The history of anthropology is filled with stories of such relationships. The movie, *The Last of His Tribe* (available in most video stores) may give you a feel for the difference between scientific and hermeneutic approaches with regard to relationships. The movie depicts the interaction of Kroeber, the scientific anthropologist, with Ishi, the last member of the Yahi tribe. Kroeber practices the scientific method in the sense that he is objective and detached with Ishi, treating him as an object of curiosity and study. However, Ishi lets Kroeber know that he wants to be a friend rather than data in Kroeber's notebook. Kroeber fears this and leaves Berkeley for an appointment in New York City. A hermeneut would realize the importance of relationships for both parties. Later, when he hears of Ishi's death, Kroeber realizes the bonding that had taken place and the harm he has done to Ishi.

Where close friendships can form, the likelihood of romance increases. More than one anthropologist has married a native met during his or her fieldwork. In a ten-week project the likelihood of long-term romance seems slight, but not impossible. We advise students to avoid romantic involvement with informants. While close friendships are beneficial—both to the people involved and to the study—a romance can cloud the study with intense emotions and ethical dilemmas.

You need to be careful in your fieldwork friendships not to break the confidentiality that you have ensured other informants. As you spend more time with your fieldwork friends, the opportunities increase for divulging information from other interviews. This usually does not involve a conscious decision and is difficult to check. You will need to become more self-conscious in this regard, for the sake of respect for others and for the success of your project.

One problem that may arise because of the bonding that occurs with certain informants is dependency. One or more informants may soon need you for your emotional support, or for favors. For example, an elderly person may ask you to do some shopping for him or her as a favor. This might soon develop into a routine that he or she expects to continue after your project is complete. Another example is a welfare mother who asks you to help her prepare for a high school equivalency exam (GED). An informant may be lonely and desperately need your company after experiencing it only a time or two. This could easily occur in studies of such groups as the elderly or seriously ill patients. These dependency relationships become a concern for the investigator when the project ends. Can you just leave the person? Will he or she become depressed? Will he or she find someone else to get prescriptions or groceries? Will he or she give up on GED aspirations? You want to be careful to pay attention as relationships intensify, particularly with those who are less socially mobile, to make certain that you are not becoming indispensable in their lives.

We find that transference can often occur during the formation of close relationships. A transference is a psychological phenomenon—a more or less unconscious emotional reaction to a person due to one's residue of emotions from experiences encountered earlier in life. The reaction one feels in a transference of past emotions may or may not be appropriate to the current situation. Many things might trigger such an emotional reaction: another person's tone of voice, turn of phrase, gesture, facial expression, or general physical appearance. Other catalysts might be included in the setting: smells, sounds, the visual scene, and/or the light level. Still other similarities with the past may lie in the circumstances: a potential power struggle, or a situation of perceived vulnerability.

Before saying more about transference, let us give you an example. One student (we will call him Dan) in his thirties experienced a transference during an interview with a high school principal in the principal's office. Dan had been expelled from high school about twenty years before by a callous and punitive principal. As the interview unfolded, many features of the setting and the informant triggered an angry transference in Dan. The layout of the office, the smell of lemon oil, the sound of a pendulum clock were all familiar. The man behind the desk reminded the student of his former principal in facial appearance, in his flippant style of speech, in gestures, in tone of voice, and in his arrogant attitude. Dan found himself getting into a heated argument with the informant, and he had to leave the scene. He told his support group later that he felt a deep hatred and loathing for the informant, even though he barely knew him. Although Dan's reaction did not suit the current scene, it is understandable when we know the injustice and humiliation Dan had experienced under very similar circumstances twenty years earlier.

Some emotional transferences are positive. We can get warm feelings for someone we have just met. Although you may be able to pick out characteristics in the other person to justify your attraction, the intensity may indicate a matching with earlier pleasant feelings. Perhaps an elderly gentleman's voice, mannerisms, and politeness (even the smell of his aftershave) unconsciously evoke feelings of kindness for your grandfather who held you on his knee when you were five years old. Psychologists have suggested that the transferences are generally more intense and uncontrollable, and are more likely unconscious, when they relate to very early childhood experiences.

We have several reasons for educating you about transference. As we have mentioned earlier, they may distort your interpretation of an informant. Negative transference may also interfere with your need to establish trusting relationships with important informants. Dan's experience with the high school principal is a clear example of a case where his interpersonal interaction was controlled by a strong negative transference. Fieldwork can reflect life in this respect. We also find that we have "personality conflicts" in other aspects of our lives. However, the need to develop open, trusting relationships with strangers makes the frequency of transference higher.

The presence of transference also increases the likelihood of emotions being stirred up during fieldwork. When the transferences are negative, the experience can be painful, or at least frustrating. Many people find that old personal and interpersonal issues keep coming to the surface due to transference or due to identification with the issues of informants. You need not shy away from these opportunities; they can lead to new insights for your journal and for your own personal growth.

Barriers to Understanding

A problem that some students experience involves not being able to discern the unique qualities that their group possesses. This problem seems to arise from two possible sources: an ethnocentrism that we call reductionism; or from the feeling that danger lurks in setting people apart as different. We would like to address these personal attitudes so that you might feel more able to collect pertinent data.

It is neither necessary, nor wise, to view others as being exactly like us in order to understand them. You may think that by assuming another is like you that you may interpret his or her every behavior, feeling, and imagining because you know what you would feel, think, or do in the same situation. This may actually reflect a self-centered view that you will want to discard. We do not know how people become more open-minded. Perhaps in this case it would be a good idea to try to foster an attitude of obsession with looking for unique and special differences among people.

CherylAnne found that because she had been taught as a child to respect people of other ethnicities by seeing them as "just like us," she had some difficulty in discerning a uniqueness in her group members. Difference between groups does not have to be derogatory—many ethnic groups celebrate their uniqueness. In many ways we are all the same because we are all human, but many if not all groups have unique characteristics. Sometimes features are subtly different. For example, an emotion such as shame may be manifested more easily or more intensely or may be interpreted differently by group members, or may be used in different contexts from the culture in which you have grown up. It takes practice to remind yourself to not automatically categorize a behavior, or a feeling, or a statement without examining it for its subtleties. Keep in mind, that people *like* to be understood in their subtleties. You are offering them respect in carrying this out.

Another place where we see self-centeredness as a psychological problem in fieldwork is with regard to projection. We have described projection earlier as the process of ascribing to others feelings and motivations that are really our own. The insidious aspect of projection is that it can be mistaken by the investigator as empathy. When empathizing you are relating the experiences of others to previous experiences of your own. You probably cannot relate their experiences to identical ones inside your memory, but there will be subtle connections. This is an important part of understanding. With projection a person replaces the other's reporting of experiences with his or her own. Such a person is really only then understanding his or her self, not the other person.

How can you detect and/or control projection? We recommend intently *listening* to the other and *asking for verification* of your understanding. Empathy requires listening to and negotiating with your informants. It requires being less self-centered and more other-centered. This can be tedious for the self-centered person. One's own interior picture of the other will need to be modified to come as close as possible to that of the informant. This takes place by questioning the informant, checking with him or her to see if one's assumptions are correct, and by offering or asking for metaphorical examples.

A lack of trust on the part of the investigator can also block understanding. We feel that the ethnographer must be trusting and must demonstrate that trust in order for an open relationship to develop with informants. This may be difficult for some of you. Prior experiences in your life may cause you to be suspicious of people and their motivations. You may fear humiliation or punishment from others if you were to contemplate exposing your feelings, weaknesses, or regrettable experiences. Yet, this kind of exposure—

making yourself vulnerable—is one of the fastest and most assured ways of establishing trust in a relationship. You might try to reduce your fear of being harmed in your openness by asking yourself what the worst scenario could be—look for details in your imagination. Then ask yourself what the likelihood is of such a scene developing. Sometimes our fears are vague and unrealistic, but we do not realize it until we try to describe them in detail.

Should you have such a fear of expressing feelings, weaknesses, or regrettable experiences, you will likely also be inhibited in speaking to your support group. You should consider making the group a place to experiment with speaking openly. Most of the group members are likely to be empathetic and to have made themselves vulnerable by being open about their feelings and shortcomings. Start with a minor risk—even admitting the fear of talking to the group. When this presents no repercussions you may want to be more bold in your risk-taking. You may soon find yourself taking similar risks with your informants.

Perhaps not so ironically, overcoming these blocks to successful hermeneutic research will also give you tools by which to improve your life's interpersonal relationships. Many students have remarked to us that hermeneutics is learning about life or is understanding people. We agree.

Exercises

6.1 In your journal, write in detail what you would imagine to be your worst scenario for an interview. After you have written it, ask yourself how likely this is to occur—write your answer. Finally, write, in detail, what you would imagine to be the best scenario for you. Return to this last description and read it before each interview.

6.2 Create examples (or use them from your own experience) to illustrate two of the following: reductionism, projection, or transference. Explain why your examples are appropriate.

Chapter 7

Data Analysis

To be surprised, to wonder, is to begin to understand.

—José Ortega y Gasset

Making generalities about the understandings of group members is both a major responsibility of ethnographers and a process fraught with difficulties. By definition, you should characterize a culture by the shared meanings of its members. Thus, culture has some structure of its own, which we define as articulable by its members. So we analyze the conversations and descriptions made by informants, looking for pieces that paint a consistent picture. This should be an ongoing process in order for ethnographers to get feedback on the pictures that they formulate in their minds as they work.

Several issues complicate this process. First of all, the ethnographer must make decisions about how well any one informant can speak for the understanding of other group members. Are certain members more coherent in their thinking, more contemplative in their reflection, more detailed and colorful in their descriptions? Are they able to represent the thoughts of others? The analyst should be able to find many similarly expressed (albeit less detailed or colorful) accounts in data from other informants.

A second complexity involves the addition of structure by the writer, added in an attempt to bridge the gap between the understandings of the people being studied and those who are to read the descriptions. Metaphors may be used to aid the ethnographer in painting the picture that the reader will take in. Danger lurks where inappropriate structures and metaphors are used in such a process. It is best to use informant metaphors as much as possible in your descriptions. You should substantiate the origins of structure and metaphor, at least as a part of the process of analysis. By portraying this process in the ethnography, you would be reassuring some of your readers.

There are several strategies that you can employ to put together the data you have been collecting. Often the strategy of arranging data can intertwine with the actual process of collecting the information. Since analysis should be an ongoing process in the hermeneutic method, it is not surprising that a strategy would influence both the collecting and the arranging of data. We suggest the following frameworks: analysis of the ideal/real culture contrast, event analysis, process analysis, emotion analysis, and metaphor analysis.

Contrasting Ideal and Real

All groups that have values, rules, and ethics teach ideals by which members should live—behaviors that they should follow whether out of the desire to do good, to avoid retribution, or to keep their social relations running smoothly. We refer to this as the group's ideal culture. At other times it is group leaders who determine the ideal culture. Sometimes it is passed down through written laws and rituals. Sometimes it is determined by most of the members of the group. We believe that all such groups also possess a real culture that includes both adherence to and exceptions to those ideals. We feel that good fieldwork will yield information about both. Examples from student fieldwork include a nursing home that describes "living the good life" in its brochures, but in reality cannot provide a meaningful existence for most of its residents. Another example is the ideal of committed relationships and refined demeanor among members of a gay community. The exceptions are flamboyant and radical members who create an undesirable image for the community. A third example is a small Asian community that ideally would like to keep their original religion and values, but most members are adopting American values because there is not enough of a community and no religious temple.

We can suggest a few hints in pursuing this approach. Keep an ear cocked for apparent exceptions to the ideal group member in the stories or accounts that are relayed to you. When you hear such apparent exceptions, ask about them. The same holds true for the behaviors of group members. For example, if members are to abstain from alcohol and you see members drinking, you should diplomatically and discreetly ask about the discrepency.

Be on the lookout for special labels and phrases that indicate either exceptions to or promoters of ideals. For exceptions you may find terms like hypocrites, losers, bums, fakes, or a phrase like "ruining it for others." Those promoting the ideals may be referred to by descriptors such as "holier than thou" or "do-gooders."

You may need to establish trust with most informants before they admit to the exceptions to their perfect society or perfect organization. Others may describe to you the balanced picture on your first meeting. If you ask the right questions you can enhance your chances of obtaining these insights. CherylAnne designed the following questions in her study and found their use successful: "What is it about your community (or culture) that you want to hand on to your children? If there was anything that you could change about your group (or culture) what would it be?" The answers to these questions quickly establish ideals and the exceptions to them. The first question does not work well for clubs, work occupations, or agencies.

We urge certain precautions in using this analysis strategy. You need to be courteous in your pursuit of the "real" culture. You could inadvertently insult the informant, a person observed by you, or all the group members by pointing out exceptions to their beliefs.

Important questions to answer are: Who set the ideals—outsiders? group members? leaders? Who is assessing the exceptions—you? one informant? many informants? Are exceptions accepted by group members—with or without retribution? What frequency are the exceptions and by what percentage of the membership? Answering these will help prevent your presentation of a misleading picture.

Event Analysis

Event analysis requires the presence of an extraordinary occurrence, that is, one that is either unique or relatively infrequent, that leads to meaningful activity or meaningful dialogue among most members of the group. This event then becomes the focal point for insightful analysis. Examples for the mass society of the U.S. include the assassination of John F. Kennedy, the Watergate scandal, the Desert Storm incursion, and the Rodney King arrest and trial. Events within the group you are studying might include the death or resignation of a leader, the loss of funding for a club or agency, a group's reorganization, a change in ownership of a company, a competitive event like a body-building competition, a graduation from the group, an initiation into the group, or an annual ceremony such as a Fourth of July parade or a tribal Sun Dance.

Sometimes events that take place in a mass society affect smaller groups in a unique way. These events may have a specific meaning for your group. Perhaps the Watergate scandal was "just like the situation now with the mayor." It will be your responsibility to puzzle out the unique way in which they relate the well-known event to their own group.

If some people are not aware of the event on which you are focusing, or if they consider the occurrence insignificant, you will need to look at these exceptions to determine if they are unique in other ways. For example, if some members of an agency do not see the appointment of a new director as important, you might find that these are members who are near retirement. The future direction of the agency might not mean much to them.

Once you feel that you have pin-pointed an event of importance to group members, you may have to go back and interview informants again. You might consider asking them why the topic of this event did not occur in earlier conversations.

Sometimes the event has passed, but memories of informants still hold the insights. Barry used an event, the 1927 coal strike, to center many questions. The result was insights into emotional practices of residents. Other events from ethnographic analyses include Edward Schieffelin's analysis of a Kaluli dance ceremony and Kai Erikson's analysis of a disastrous flood. The Kaluli *Gisaro* ceremony causes sorrow and anger in the guests for whom it is performed. The dancers expect to be burned by members of their audience. In elucidating the natives' understanding of this ritual Schieffelin came to understand their spiritual beliefs, their practice of reciprocity, their relationships, and their emotions. Erikson interviewed survivors of a flood that washed away towns and killed scores of people on the Appalachian Plateau of West Virgina. He learned about their kin and community relations, their sense of place, and their history of passivity in the face of the coal-mining industry.

There are a few precautions for you to consider in using this approach. At times you may have to be careful to determine which aspect of a series of events is most significant to group members. Thus, you may need to know if a local crime or the subsequent trial is most significant to group members, or if the group treasurer's misuse of funds or his or her resignation is more significant.

It may be helpful for you to classify an event into one of three categories: participatory, observed, or news event. Using a brawl at a ballgame as an example, you may find that some group members experienced the brawl, that is, were involved in it. Another possibility is that some group members witnessed it firsthand. The third possibility is that some members learned of the event by word-of-mouth or through news sources. All will have their interpretations of the event, but the category of the experience may affect the interpretations. We suggest that you keep these distinctions in mind.

If you analyze a cyclical event—that is, one that occurs yearly or more frequently, you will need to ensure that the event has not become routine and/or lacking in meaning. For example, for many Americans holidays like Memorial Day and Labor Day have become mere three-day weekends, devoid of their original meaning.

If you begin this type of analysis while conducting the fieldwork, you need to be careful to not lead the informants into thinking an event is significant when for them it was not. Bring up the topic in general terms and see if they specifically mention the event. If they do not, you may bring it up. However, you should note in your report that it had required your bringing it up. If you think that the death of a specific leader is important, you might begin questioning their thoughts about leadership. If you think that the loss of institutional funding was an important event, you might open up a conversation about funding.

Process Analysis

Somewhat related to event analysis is the technique of process analysis. A process is a transformation that takes place over a length of time, a gradual and enduring change in values, traditions, policy, method, or thinking. It could come about through a series of events, by the change in the policy of a company or government agency, by a change in technology, or by a change in economics.

Examples include the process of westernization of specific indigenous peoples that has been studied by many ethnographers. For example, Conrad Kottack has written about social change in a Brazilian fishing village in the context of forces such as industrialization, urbanization, tourism, and mass media. Likewise, Eder has written about the social stress on the Batak, an indigenous culture of the Philippines. He focuses on the interaction of their culture with the outside world.

Another example is Barry's study of the process of mechanization in the coal mines. As he questioned retired miners about how the nature of their jobs had changed, he learned about the group's work values.

As was the case with event analysis, studying processes requires you to ask yourself if the change is really significant to your informants or if *you* have emphasized the change, making it the focus because you know that it will be significant to your audience.

Emotion Analysis

The study of emotions can always be an element of any ethnographic study. Here, we present it as the central focus of analysis. Although these do not exhaust the possibilities for studies of emotion, we will describe three analytic approaches to emotions: emotional understandings, emotional acts, and nonverbal indicators of emotions during interviews.

Informants may present clues to their understandings of emotions during their descriptions of fellow group members, or members of other groups or of themselves. These include their ideas of what gives rise to certain emotions, what, if anything, can be done to change a mood or an emotional reaction, and what are appropriate and inappropriate emotions for a given situation. You may be able to relate these to group values and philosophy. For example, a religious group may believe that it takes two or more years for an initiate to be fully converted to their doctrine. Long-term members may be chastised by the congregation for feeling a suspicious fear of religious authority. The congregation may, however, tolerate such feelings in "newcomers." Thus, this group displays conditions of acceptable and unacceptable emotions in its members.

Emotions may also be analyzed as behaviors. People are more often likely to display a behavior when in an emotional state than they are to say: "I feel angry" or "I feel ashamed." Are some of these indicators of emotions unique for the group under study? For example, is it acceptable or unacceptable to commit the emotional act of breaking valuable objects as a sign of anger or of cutting one's hair as a sign of mourning? Can these acts be understood in the context of expressed group values or philosophy? Can these emotional acts have other messages or consequences? For example, does breaking objects in anger intimidate other group members? Ask and you may find out.

You may discover during interviews that nonverbal language suggests emotions being experienced by the informants. These include sarcasm in the voice as a possible sign of resentment, an elevated volume of speech as a sign of anger, a dry mouth (or conversely excessive salivation) as signs of nervousness, a quivering voice as a sign of sadness or an averted gaze as a sign of shame. Asking the informant if they feel nervous, sad, or resentful will both provide a check on your reading of nonverbal cues *and* provide an opening for further discussion. This can be true even if the informant indicates that you misread his or her feelings. He or she may state the true feeling or, if not, you may ask.

We recommend several precautions in pursuing this line of analysis. Be discreet and sensitive in your pursuit of information on emotions. It is easy to offend others and to misunderstand them—this is a very likely area for your projection of *your* feelings into the analysis. Be especially careful to check with informants about nonverbal cues—these are easily misinterpreted. Avoid judgmental evaluations of your group's emotions and emotional behaviors. It is better to describe them as unique or as different from those of mass culture.

Metaphor

Entire books have been written about the metaphor and its importance in anthropology. We have found metaphor to be an invaluable tool in everyday communication as well as in anthropological fieldwork. While it is not our purpose to define or analyze the various forms and usage of tropes (others, more qualified, have already tackled that awesome task), we would like to suggest some points on which to reflect when presented with a metaphor in your fieldwork.

You likely learned in English composition class that metaphor is figurative language in which a word or phrase is used to denote a likeness between its literal meaning and another object or idea. But what does that mean? We use metaphorical language daily, and like the grammatical rules and structures of our native language, we use metaphors often without recognizing that we are using them. Simply stated, metaphors present concrete images, sensory information; they may attribute human or animal characteristics to an object or idea, or attribute inanimate qualities to a living being; they are substitutions used to offer color, clarity, and description in order to enhance our understanding. A friend once used a metaphor to explain metaphor, saying: "Metaphor is like a bridge across a chasm. A person on one side of the chasm extends a 'bridge' (metaphor) to a person on the other side, whereby the receiver can cross the chasm, and by crossing, joins the sender in understanding."

During the course of CherylAnne's study of Mexican immigrant women, she had one notable experience with metaphor. In a third interview with Carla, an informant with whom she had become friends, she told CherylAnne: "This house is like a prison to me." A while later she said: "I feel like a prisoner within my own home." Her comments stunned CherylAnne, not only because of the emotive power of the imagery, but because it shattered the heretofore held conviction that Carla personified the "happy homemaker," content in her traditional role as wife and mother.

The metaphorical "bridge" that Carla offered to the ethnographer was an invitation to join her in a deeper understanding of her situation. She had challenged CherylAnne's understanding, and that challenge required that the investigator examine the "prison" metaphor closely, both in the *context* in which it was presented, and in its *limitations*.

CherylAnne felt that she intuitively understood what Carla meant by "prison/prisoner" at the time she spoke. Later, when reflecting on her field notes, she could see that it was the content of the surrounding conversation that clarified the message. They had been talking about how Carla's life in the United States compared to her life in Mexico. Her lack of English kept her from getting a job here and developing a wide circle of friends—both of which she had in Mexico. The language barrier created for her a situation of intense isolation in which the only conversation/companionship she found occurred within the walls of her home, with her husband and children. The context in which the metaphor occurred is of the utmost importance in interpreting its meaning. Imagine what a different interpretation CherylAnne might have come to had the "prison/prisoner" metaphor occurred in a conversation about traditional Hispanic male dominance, for example, or U.S. policies dealing with illegal immigrants!

In reaching an understanding with your informant, it is important not to extend the meaning of the metaphor beyond that which the informant intended. While some metaphors can be expanded into multifaceted allegories where several parallels can be drawn between a real-life situation and the metaphorical "picture," others are intended to illustrate one simple idea. In Carla's case, the metaphor was not intended to allude to any warden, guards, or fellow-inmates; there were no bars on her windows, no real physical restraints on her freedom; she had no sense of punishment or of "doing time." The prison metaphor was limited to her sense of isolation as a result of the language barrier. In order to avoid overextending a metaphor, you can let the metaphor suggest further questions to ask your informant, and thereby determine how the *informant* is limiting the metaphor's meaning.

Often we jump to a conclusion in interpreting a metaphor, a conclusion based on our preconceived notions, culturally limited experience, or idiomatic expression peculiar to our own language or social group. We use metaphoric language so often within our own group of peers that we may fail to recognize that a metaphor expressed by a member of another culture or by a member of a distinct subgroup within our own society may have an entirely different meaning. Consider what the word "prison" might mean to a habitual criminal who has been in and out of "the system" most of his or her life, as compared to a person who has no law-breaking experience and is horrified at the thought of incarceration.

The unique worldview of a specific culture or group must be taken into account when interpreting metaphors. Take for example, the "oyster and the pearl." Without giving you a context, if we were to suggest that something were "like an oyster and a pearl," many would interpret that metaphor to mean that the other "thing" was unattractive in appearance, common, and without much worth, out of which came a rare object of beauty and value. Another interpretation from the same peer group might focus on the common oyster's lengthy labor to produce the tiny treasure. But what if your informant came from a culture with a worldview that placed little or no value on "pretty baubles"; who revered, above all, living creatures; who had no word for "work" or "labor," perceiving all activities as equal in pleasure and effort? If a member of this other culture were to liken something to an oyster and a pearl, you would need to ask more questions in order to discover your informant's true meaning.

Any one of your informants may turn out to be somewhat of a poet or, at least, a creative thinker. For that reason, any metaphor offered in an interview should not be taken at face value, but explored through further questions. In a hermeneutic study, we are often asking our informants philosophical, thought-provoking questions; questions that are not easily answered. Some of the metaphorical "bridges" your informants offer you may occur spontaneously within the conversation; others may be the product of lengthy reflection on the part of your informant. So while metaphors often reflect cultural norms, a creative mind might infuse a tired metaphor with a fresh new meaning.

If the same metaphor is presented by two or more of your informants, it may represent a shared understanding among the group you are studying. Colorful metaphors often become part of the slang of a specific community, and such idiomatic expressions may offer a unifying "thread" that ties the responses of different informants, and indicates a common perspective that is shared by the group.

George Lakoff and Mark Johnson have suggested in their writing that metaphor is more than a matter of poetic imagination, rhetorical flourish, and a characteristic of language. They view human conceptual systems as fundamentally metaphorical in nature. As such, cultural metaphors largely affect the way we think, the way we perceive, and even what we do every day. We believe that Lakoff and Johnson present a convincing case for this thesis. A group may create metaphors to communicate understanding among themselves. These may also tend to channel thinking in certain directions. An example that Lakoff and Johnson used is the concept of time as money, something to be spent, saved, invested, borrowed, lost, and traded. To what extent are we limited in thinking of time in any other way? Assuming that metaphors have this function, we believe that students should search for the unique metaphors used by cultural members. These should provide insights into cultural understandings.

Metaphors can be challenging to your fieldwork—they certainly can be enlightening. They color our conversation, indeed our lives, with flashes of insight that result in the satisfaction of understanding another's viewpoint. Tread carefully on the "bridges" that are offered to you during your fieldwork, and never ignore them. They may offer some of the most poignant surprises in your negotiations of understanding.

INDEXING FOR ANALYSIS

You may be wondering about how one goes about carrying out the analysis—what are the steps or practices. We recommend marking your journal and field notes with an ink of contrasting color. You will need to underline important statements, descriptions, and self-reflections. These include repeated phrases and repeated terms. Why do these hold so much weight in informant's talk? Likewise, you will need to underline unusual terms or any unusual use of common terms. Of course, metaphors should be marked, particularly fresh, unique ones.

Star those areas of interviews that contain detailed descriptions of behaviors, practices, rituals, or beliefs. Also mark passages in which an informant is able to remember exact dates or exact policy of an organization.

Other important material might include statements involving emotions. This can include emotion talk; for example, how someone must feel or a judgment of someone because of the way they feel, or a description of how the informant is feeling. Emotional talk is different, but is also worth noting. What topics seem to excite the person, anger the person, bring joy to the person?

You should mark those cases of apparent contradictions in informant reports. This may occur in two separate conversations from one informant or from two different informants. It is best in inquiring into these with a group member, to have the attitude of resolving what may not really be contradictions.

Another sort of marking is topic indexing. Read through your data and write down the various topics discussed, and the frequency of their appearance. Then design symbols to represent each topic. Here is a short example:

# = envy	* = techniques of farming	@ = childhood
$ = money concerns	% = farm community	+ = work ethic
& = romance	W = women's issues	! = regret

Then go back through your notes and mark those areas where the topics occur by placing a symbol in the margin. You will need to do the same with your journal, using additional symbols.

Some of you will be using archival material as well as field notes. In this category we include newspaper, magazine, and journal articles, an organization's brochure, descriptive brochures and educational brochures, notes from training sessions (for volunteer organizations), music, films, photographs, oaths, rules, and book excerpts. An ideal way to tie these into the analysis is to use the same set of indexing symbols to mark this material.

Once material is indexed, you can make passes through your field and archival notes for each topic, writing down short descriptions of important data. How much uniformity and variability do you see? You may need to perform this type of analysis only once if you are carrying out a ten-week project while attending classes. For longer projects (for example, a seven-day-a-week summer project) you will need to do this periodically to get a feel for what questions need to be answered in future interviews. Especially relevant are seeming contradictions and avoided topics. You will want to ask yourself (and future informants) why certain subjects that seem relevant don't come up.

The analysis schemes mentioned earlier in the chapter may prove helpful once data is arranged by indexed topics. As ideas come to your mind, jot them down. This way a theme or organizational scheme may pop into your mind. At this stage you are ready to begin writing. Before we begin describing the process, we want to bring to your awareness some of the ethical issues involved in ethnographic fieldwork.

Exercises

7.1 Based on the information from chapter 7 and using five to seven of your interviews, do the following:
   a. design a topic index of at least five elements;
   b. speculate on a possible analysis strategy (even though this may be a little early for it).

7.2 Read an account written by an "insider," for example a magazine article or a letter to the editor of a periodical to discover a significant metaphor that increases your understanding of the group (or person). Write down the metaphor and your understanding.

7.3 Write at least one possible event and one possible process that you anticipate might have been, is currently, or will be experienced by your chosen group.

7.4 One strategy for finding both focus and theme in a study is clustering. Clustering is a free-writing exercise whose purpose is to bring some kind of order to the array of data, concepts, and ideas generated by your fieldwork. It can also prove useful as a tool to determine a focus or to narrow the focus of a study that is too broad in its scope. Your web of entries will appear heavy in one or more areas, scanty in others.

In the center of a blank sheet of paper write the name of the group you have chosen to study, and circle it. In the surrounding area, write what you consider to be major subheadings of information generated by your study. Write these in the form of single words or phrases. Next, give yourself complete freedom as you jot down words and phrases that describe the data you have collected. Key informants' names (or codes) may surface at this point along with the specific insights or challenges they presented. Circle each entry and draw lines between the "bubbles" that have a relationship to each other. As you draw these connecting lines your diagram will begin to resemble a complex web of concepts and data.

Chapter 8

ETHICS

When we object to one person's using another what we are saying (at least some of the time) is that something that is not a mere good or commodity is being treated as one.

—*Nancy Davis*

Since sociology and anthropology involve direct research with human subjects, these disciplines need to be concerned about the ethics of their fieldwork practices. This chapter concerns itself with the issue of acceptable and unacceptable practices and with the rationale that underlies this distinction. As we have mentioned throughout the book, the hermeneutic method requires us to become intimate with informants in order to negotiate an understanding with them.

If you think about the relationships that you have with your friends you will realize that you have certain obligations to them. As relationships evolve, they become more personal. With this deepening of friendship, you and your friends expect more openness and trust. In relationships such as these, if you concealed your feelings, it would be a form of deception and a betrayal of trust. There is a deepening of relationship as one comes to understand another. Your feelings grow for the person—your friend—and you need to become more considerate in your behavior.

As you do hermeneutic fieldwork, you will develop deep relationships with your informants. You need to prove worthy of trust in order for them to share their feelings, beliefs, and opinions with you. Sometimes you will need to initiate openness with them to show that you trust them. As you come back to them for more information, the relationships deepen—even over the course of a semester-length project, many students have found that they developed one or more close friendships with informants.

In one way these relationships are unique from other friendships—you are relying on them for something that will benefit you at the same time that you are empathetically listening to their personal accounts. This need not lead to any contradiction in your feelings or behaviors, but it can. Luckily, there is a simple ethical principle that you can follow to guide your actions: persons should be treated at all times as ends in themselves, never merely as means to an end. This is the ethical principle of Immanuel Kant and it refers to treating others as people, not as objects to be manipulated for our own benefit. We should not *use* people, but rather respect them as unique beings and personalities.

To us, this concern for informants as ends in themselves involves several issues: the disclosure of the project to informants; the honoring of informant privacy; the process of giving to as well as taking from the relationship; the effect of published results on the group; and the power dynamics during interview, analysis, and writing.

Disclosure—Avoiding Deception

You will need to practice disclosure in order to show respect for the informants' dignity and to build trust. You should disclose the nature of the project, that is, the purpose, the intended audience, and the techniques to be used. You should briefly describe hermeneutic analysis. For example, you might say that you want to *understand* group members' perspective by talking with them about certain topics. Indicate likely topics and the likelihood of any change in topics as the project progresses. Let them know who will read your notes and to whom you will talk about your experiences. Assure them of anonymity, and describe your coding system to ensure privacy.

Light and Kleiber have drawn attention to the possibility of disclosing all field notes to informants as well as analyses of data. In their study they were "insiders" studying a women's health cooperative; thus, this form of disclosure had definite ethical ramifications. In their orientation to medical self-help, this group emphasized the importance of shared knowledge and power and opposed a medical professionalism that defines information as a property of the few. This philosophy of shared knowledge and power and exclusion of privileged professional information rather easily transferred to the conditions of the anthropological investigation. After an initial period in which the investigators were secretive in their data gathering and analyses, they were challenged by collective members seeking a mutual openness between the investigators and those being investigated. Both sides felt a vulnerability in giving out inside knowledge about themselves.

Once the agreement was made to share power and knowledge, interview transcripts were kept in easily accessible files at the health collective offices. No one exclusively owned it. The data sharing agreement worked well here because of the underlying philosophy of the cooperative and because all members liked and respected one another. They had much in common with other members: age, gender, social class, and sociopolitical outlooks. Also, the group was relatively small (20 to 25 members). Any analyses, criticisms, and suggestions were meant in good faith and accepted that way. The rules of the cooperative included an openness and sharing by all members—including the investigators.

Should the same ethical practices hold for any study using the hermeneutic method? Since openness and sharing are characteristics of the interpersonal negotiation of truth that takes place in close relationships with informants, it seems that we should share data and analyses. However, as we mentioned in chapter five, often the group is too incoherent or suspicious for this to take place. Because your project will be less extensive than graduate school research, we do not recommend attempting this level of sharing in your study. Most groups are content with being offered the opportunity to read your final report.

Make certain to inform them of your plans for the final report—will it be available for reading by all group members? Would you like to publish it? Think carefully about these questions because it may have a heavy influence on the group members' decision about participating.

Since the late 1970s colleges and universities have become concerned about the need for the consent of people to be studied. Sadly, the schools' incentive for having such a concern has been more one of fear of lawsuit than one of ethical principle. Even so, subjects are now in a position of improved protection from eavesdroppers. Investigators now must clearly indicate the nature and purpose of their study to each individual being studied. Furthermore, each person to be studied must consent to being a part of the project.

Your school should have a human subjects policy and a committee to administer it. If your instructor has not mentioned these, you should inquire of your instructor concerning the policy rules. We will relay information about programs with which we are familiar. Your policy will likely be similar.

Your professor should have requested approval from the school's human subjects committee prior to the beginning of the course. The chief purpose of its policy is to shift responsibility to the professor or individual investigators (i.e., students) to indicate to subjects of investigation the probability of physical, psychological, or social injury and to gain permission to use information obtained from the subject. This policy also ensures the autonomy (i.e., independence) of the participant (or potential participant). He or she may choose not to participate given risks to health, relationships and privacy.

The personnel at Mesa State College must adhere to the following guidelines to protect human rights and welfare of participants:

The investigator must:

1. Ensure that participants receive clear, thorough explanations prior to consenting to participate in research.
2. Ensure that participants will not be exposed to physical, psychological, or social injury as a result of participating in the research.
3. Respect rights and privacy of participants and assure that maximum confidentiality of personal information will be maintained.
4. Weigh the inherent risks compared to the projected benefits that will be derived from the research.

Informed consent will include, in the form of a cover letter or introductory paragraph:

1. Brief description of purpose of research/survey. In cases where disclosure of the purpose of the research/survey might create subject bias, the researcher may elect to give a partial statement prior to participation and complete the description after data collection.

2. Description of what participant will be asked to do.
3. Assurance that participant may decline to participate or withdraw from research at any time.
4. In the case of (experimental) research: request for signature, signifying initial and subsequent consent to participate in the research.

In the case of a survey (including hermeneutic interviews): if the respondent agrees to participate and respond to questions, the participant should be informed that responding to the questions implies that consent to participate has been given.

Faculty must submit a short proposal and request ten working days prior to needing approval. Faculty are responsible for student projects.

With regard to consent, you will be able to carry this out by typing a short description of your project and methods. We suggest referring to a "project" rather than a "study." The concept that many people hold of a study is one of a scientific process. By using the term "project" you are less likely to misinform and put off potential informants.

We have concluded that verbal consent—"Yes, I'll be a part of your project"—is the best means of obtaining consent while maintaining anonymity. We say this because once a consent form is signed and handed to a committee, the participant's name is available for reading by others (perhaps not at your discretion) and for possible connection with the final report or field notes. Based on this argument, we suggest that you read your project description to the potential informants or have them read it. Then ask if they are willing to participate.

One situation in ethnographic analysis deserves special consideration with regard to disclosure—participant-observation. Participant-observation is the technique of blending in with the natives in such a way that they begin to behave in a natural manner in your presence. The traditional goal of this technique has been to observe this natural behavior because it will reveal truths that the natives would ordinarily deny or of which they are unconscious. Some investigators consider this method to reveal the "real culture," as opposed to the "ideal culture" expressed in native's beliefs. Usually for this technique to work, the natives must be unaware that the investigator is recording their behaviors. The best way (perhaps the only way) to achieve this is through deception.

By not mentioning the method of participant-observation or by mentioning only that he or she is doing an anthropological study, the investigator can practice this technique without the informants' full awareness. In this case, the investigator is not deceptive about being an anthropologist; however, he or she *is* deceptive about the techniques being employed. This clearly involves an invasion of informant's privacy, and as Davis has pointed out, the question of whether privacy has been invaded can shade into the question of whether people are being used. We need to be open and honest to treat people as ends in themselves.

Related to participant-observation is the practice of analyzing conversation that occurs during "frame-breaks." Breaking frame is the practice by which one participant in a dialogue (particularly the informant during an ethnographic interview) abruptly changes the line of conversation. This could involve the appearance of a third party with whom the informant speaks. During this time, should their conversation be considered data? It might also involve personal or friendly conversation between the investigator and the informant that the informant did not consider to be part of the interview. For example, the friendly conversation before the recognized interview starts, the "chitchat" that follows the questions or an interspersed personal statement by the informant that might relate to current political or personal issues spoken out of nervousness or out of the need for a listening ear. A phone call to the informant that interrupts the interview is a third illustration of a frame-break. Should you use this information? It seems to us that using frame-breaks as data without specifically informing the interviewee constitutes a type of deception. Deception either destroys a trusting relationship or prevents a relationship from forming. This is another case where the ethnographer would be using the informant as a means for personal gain.

How could this be avoided? We feel that every native whose actions or conversations are to be used as data should be told in detail of the method of data collecting and should be reminded of this during times when particularly sensitive or private information is being gathered. Such reminders are not rude.

Some students have expressed their guilt feelings over collecting data that may not have been entirely understood by the participants. Should this happen to you, we suggest that you keep the following considerations in mind: (1) intent is an important factor. At the time of the data collection did you *intend* to deceive anyone? If not, then you should not feel guilty. (2) Allowing everyone involved to read the report drafts would give them an opportunity to state their dissatisfaction with some information being exposed.

A dilemma arises here for investigators with certain epistemological beliefs. Those who consider "natural behavior" to be indicative of truth about a group must make a choice: either be truthful in his or her ethical behavior or gain "truth" through analysis of "natural behavior" data. In other words, he or she must choose between being deceptive in order to observe natural behavior and being truthful to informants and rely on both behavior that is more self-conscious and on natives' dialogue. We call this the "epistemological/ethical dilemma": sacrificing "truth" for the sake of ethics or sacrificing ethics for the sake of "truth." There should be no such dilemma for those who believe that reality is understood intersubjectively and that the investigator and the informants must negotiate this understanding between themselves. Natural behavior for them is then little more than a topic of conversation; there is no ethical problem.

We would like to use a few paragraphs to redefine, and even rename participant-observation. We prefer the label "cultural immersion," that is, surrounding oneself with the cultural ambiance. We see this technique as forming two important, and respectful, functions in doing hermeneutic research. It provides a method for gaining the trust and respect of informants. By being willing to experience their lives more fully you are giving the indication that their interests and enjoyments are worthy of being shared. The actual sharing, of having something in common, becomes a thread binding you to them.

Perhaps of even more importance is the experiential information that you will gain. By this, we mean that you may experience firsthand the sights, sounds, smells, tactile sensations, rhythms, timing, and perhaps urgency of events in their lives. In short, you will be getting a "feel" for what it is like to be a group member. The reason to gain such information is to better pose relevant questions to informants. You will be able to ask: "Do you feel sadness when such an event occurs?" Or you will be able to say: "I felt anxious just before the final event—do you usually feel that way?" You might also ask about the presence of certain sounds or smells, the hardness of the bench you had to sit on, or the confusing pace of an event. There are too many aspects of this technique to cover here. For further details you should read chapter 11.

We recognize two types of cultural immersion: primary and secondary. In the primary type, the investigator becomes a true member of the group. He or she genuinely wants to be a rodeo rider, a counseled client, or a dieter. Other memberships might include: a church member, a club member, a coal miner, a competitive weightlifter, a *curandero*, a migrant worker, or a ranch hand.

In carrying out secondary cultural immersion, the investigator becomes a participant in the overall scene of the group, though not a group member. So, if you wanted to study exotic dancers, you might become a waitress in an establishment that employs them. Other possibilities would include an office employee in a coal-mining company; an audience member for a rodeo; a church attendant; or a volunteer to help AIDS patients. Often this secondary engagement is more suitable, particularly for short-term projects.

"Give and Take"

Ethics can also be involved with regard to uneven exchange in the ethnographic process. Students frequently express a feeling of guilt because they are getting interviews from these people, but they are not giving anything in return. Some ethnographers have solved this problem by helping out the group with any problem they might be having. Examples of ways in which you might help the group that you are studying include: facilitating the opportunity for a group member to speak in your professors' classes. Trainers of volunteers are good representatives in providing valuable data on current social issues such as AIDS, care of the elderly, juvenile detention, gay rights, teen violence, teen pregnancy, suicide, or drug and alcohol abuse. The range in help might include physical labor (e.g., help with moving into a new facility or occasionally providing rides), arbitration (e.g., decreasing tension between staff and clients by increasing communication), explanation of the bureaucracy (e.g., helping migrant workers find needed services), or even advocacy work in which the ethnographer works for protection of the group's rights. Students often become volunteers for groups they study, such as hospice, AIDS groups, or youth services. One student in a methods class began an art program in the detention center that she studied. Another student helped an informant prepare for her GED exam.

Another answer to this feeling of guilt is that often in recording what people say, in being interested in their descriptions, and in asking informants to validate their understandings, an ethnographer is filling an important need of the group, that is, the need to be heard, and is validating the importance of their existence by helping to add coherence to the meaning of their lives. Perhaps Nancy Scheper Hughes (1992) has stated this most meaningfully when she wrote: "Seeing, listening, touching, recording can be, if done with care and sensitivity, acts of fraternity and sisterhood, acts of solidarity. Above all, they are the work of recognition."

You should also give ethical consideration to the effects of published analyses. Because hermeneutics involves understanding the members of other groups, it is not likely to lead to a publication that blames the victims for any adverse situations they experience. However, descriptions of alcoholism, physical or sexual abuse, or bigotry by group members may have adverse consequences: lowered opinion of the group by members of the public, and possible political ramifications. We hope that your sensitivity to this issue and your seeking review of written drafts by group members would minimize this concern. Often, the way something is written greatly affects the way it is perceived.

Power and Posture

Power relations between the investigator and his or her informants can pose both ethical and epistemological problems. We see these problems as involving the "posture" that the investigator takes in both the interview and the analysis stages. By posture we are referring to an attitude, a vantage point, a sense of comparative worth. You might try imagining how an investigator might stand in talking to an informant: Is the picture one of looking down on the person from a height? Is it one of the investigator wearing his or her credentials on his or her chest? Is it one of aggressiveness and persistence? This is just an image—an exaggerated stereotype, but it symbolizes an attitude of arrogance. This attitude includes feeling superior in importance, in charge of the project, and able to define the issues.

Contrast that image to one in which investigator and informant are of the same height, the investigator appears respectful and cautious not to offend the other, the investigator's voice is soft, all statements from him or her end with a rising inflection as if the statement were a question, he or she asks permission to sit, to take notes, to change a line of questioning. He or she genuinely listens. This attitude includes feeling lucky to get the cooperation of the informant, being careful to not offend, and being interested in having the informant define the issues. This stereotype is one of humility. Perhaps adding the image of Asian bowing would make the posture even more understandable.

These postures of arrogance and humility help us to define the problems related to power relations in fieldwork. The problems are those of deciding the agenda, imposing an interpretation, and objectifying the people. If the investigator chooses the agenda for discussion and ignores attempts by informants to choose the topic(s) for conversation then he or she is in an arrogant, domineering posture. The epistemological implication is that the knowledge gained may well be structured and defined by the investigator before the informant speaks, or regardless of the informant's viewpoint. Think of it this way: How powerful would a person have to be to stop a steamroller? It is also possible that the requested information is irrelevant to the informant's experiences. If the investigator is in an arrogant posture, how would he or she ever know if the question is relevant to the group members?

Separate from the issue of epistemology is the effect on the group members. Has the ethnographer offended the people? Has he or she left them feeling frustrated at not truly being heard or shocked by the bluntness and rudeness of the questions? Has the investigator worn out his or her welcome, killing any chance at a second interview? Has he or she given the ethnographic process a black eye?

You need to consider these epistemological and ethical questions before going into an interview. Talk to yourself; tell yourself that you need to be considerate and sensitive. You might actually try softening your voice and bowing as a preinterview exercise in posturing. Remind yourself that you want to know these people as ends in themselves, not as mere means to an end. Getting to know them as people with their own agendas should not jeopardize your need for a good grade—it should benefit it.

This does not mean that you can never have *your* questions. However, you should be able to ask them comfortably and with full consent of your informants. Many will acknowledge that they do not know what to tell you and ask you for questions. However, be ever alert for their agenda, should it begin to creep into the conversations.

You also need to be aware of your posture during analysis. It is easy to impose an interpretation on your data rather than listening to the natives' explanation. You, as the analyst, have the power to make this decision, and as was the case with interviewing, you hold epistemology and ethics hanging in the balance. Where does truth lie on the summary end of analysis—with the group or with the ethnographer? How will the group members feel if they never hear of your conclusions or if they strongly disagree with your conclusions? Barry's interpretation of the power issue between miners and coal companies when the industry increased supervision did not represent some informants' views. One informant strongly expressed his feelings about being misinterpreted: "Some of those handloaders, I'm sure, would resent it, if what you said were brought up to them." Of course, seeking their feedback is a characteristic of a humble posture.

Objectification

Objectifying people is a characteristic of an arrogant posture and is an indication of using someone as a means to an end. What is objectification? It is a process in which you begin to treat your data as something detached from your informants. Data manipulation and analysis can feel like number-crunching—even when qualitative methods are employed. Techniques such as those described in chapter 7, which are necessary for analysis, gives one the feeling that he or she is playing with a deck of cards, rather than understanding other people's meaning system. Perhaps this is inescapable during brief periods of the analysis. You should take care to not let the attitude slip into the process of writing. Remember the experiences we mentioned earlier of Kroeber with Ishi.

Some techniques we suggest to keep oneself "humanistic" and humble during this process are: (1) keeping in contact with some informants during the analysis and writing phases. They will be constant reminders of relationships with real people, and (2) reading over your anecdotes and good interviews during these phases. This process calls back to mind the human feelings that you felt as a consequence of your relationship with your friends.

Remember, people rarely wish to be objects of study or objects of curiosity. Anthropologists have worn out their welcome on Indian reservations because of this very phenomenon. Your informants will be especially annoyed if you, as an apparently trusting and concerned friend, treat them in this manner.

Now that we have dealt with these ethical issues, you may want to go back to earlier chapters to see how these considerations integrate into the instructions on how to do fieldwork. The concept of posture can be applied even to the theory chapters (1 and 2), as well as to the chapter on data analysis (7), and journals and field notes (5). We have reached a point where you can now consider the aspect of writing up results.

Exercise

8.1 A student ethnographer studying a disadvantaged group was puzzled concerning what to do about some information that she collected during her study. In one of her interviews her informant received a phone call during which the informant used several ethnic slurs as well as derogatory comments about ethnic groups. Later, while doing participant-observation at a community festival she again overheard several derogatory comments about some ethnic groups. In looking back over her interviews following fieldwork she noticed some comments that could possibly be interpreted as derogatory to ethnic groups. The emphasis of her study dealt with the meaning of class, government, schooling, and authority to this disadvantaged group. Write a short essay suggesting a solution.

Chapter 9

Writing

The problem of the value of truth presented itself before us—or was it we who presented ourselves before the problem?

—Friedrich Nietzche

This chapter concerns the transformation of all of your field data, journal entries, and analyses into a report. One thing that we would like to suggest from the outset is that you begin writing before your fieldwork ends. It would be good to have two more interviews after a sizable amount of the first draft has been written. We recommend this because writing often brings up new questions or exposes obvious "holes" in the study.

The process that we describe here differs from the traditional ethnographic writing process in which the investigator (usually a graduate student) returns to the United States after a year in a foreign culture to begin writing his or her report (usually a dissertation). In that case, the ethnographer is immersed in the culture and is tied mentally and emotionally into the foreign worldview while collecting data. Writing is an academic activity requiring an entirely different mental and emotional setting. Crapanzano has gone so far as to say that the investigator needs to reconstitute him- or herself as an academician on return, the self being transformed and/or fragmented in the field. Although you may feel somewhat stressed with balancing your field project and other life demands, you are not likely to feel the "culture shock" of returning from long-term fieldwork.

By beginning the writing process early you keep one foot in the world of your group and one in the world of academic pursuit. Using this process you may also be able to show the early draft of your report to some informants for feedback. This act of soliciting feedback is always rewarding: If the informants agree with what you have written it is heartwarming, if they disagree, you have some fresh, valuable insights during the writing period. When informants disagree, you have several ways to present the opposing natives' viewpoint. You might simply rewrite the analysis (we realize that rewriting is never simple) to ensure that it represents your new understanding. Remember to indicate the number of people interviewed either directly in the body of the paper or in a footnote. Readers should have a sense of how many people contributed to your understanding.

A second approach to presenting feedback from informant reviews would involve writing about your initial misconceptions and how they were clarified by the review process to yield a new understanding. Yet a third possibility would be to present both your initial view in detail and the revised view necessitated by informant review. This third option, while especially useful for giving a fuller view of the group to your readers and for illustrating a dramatic change in your view, is a difficult strategy to pursue because you will need to take great care not to mislead or confuse your readers.

What techniques and approaches can you use in writing your final report? We especially recommend the approaches of a unifying theme, collage, and painting yourself into the picture. We describe these and others below.

Unifying Theme

Often, a student is able to use a unifying theme to organize the report. If this is the case for you, you may be able to use a symbol, a metaphor, a concept, or a quote as a running idea throughout the paper. You might picture this as a bright stripe of color running through a patchwork quilt. Some examples include Clifford Geertz's use of the concept of masculinity in his essay on the Balinese cockfight, Joseph Jorgenson's use of the concept of power in his book on the Ute Sun Dance and Nancy Scheper-Hughes's use of the concept of everyday violence in her study of a Brazilian barrio, and Barry's use of the symbol of "the little man," a concept expressed often by his Pennsylvania informants, to tie together elements in one chapter of his book. The following excerpts indicate how he used the concept of "the little man" as a unifying theme:

> It was during this time that "the little man" struggled to maintain dignity in the face of destitution, exploitation, and coercion. For most it seemed like a time when displaying any sense of anger or rebelliousness was self-defeating. The younger generation saw this powerlessness as a part of being "the little man" . . . For one man it translated into a hopelessness: "You'd think that you were growin' up to be nothing. There was no light up ahead. Always you had that fear."
>
> They still undoubtedly saw themselves as "little men" when compared to the power, affluence, and autonomy of the operators, but they could collectively make themselves heard, could seek to be understood and respected, and could defy the company by striking. The "little man" would act so as to be heard and respected outside the community."

As another strategy, you may want to use various data to help "paint a general picture" and then use a case study of one informant to further illustrate a unifying theme. Some recent book-length ethnographies have followed the opposite strategy—using a biographical form to pull in more general elements about the culture. Karen McCarthy Brown's *Mama Lola* and Marjorie Shostak's *Nisa* are good examples of these. If your ethnographic essay is about East Asian refugees fighting to maintain traditional values, you might describe what you have learned of many of their treasured values, their frustrations of living in America, and intergenerational differences among refugees. Then you might write a short biographical account of one informant's migration, living experiences, frustrations, and feelings.

Using Mystery

Try to keep the reader interested and alert by using techniques such as posing questions that you later answer. This can vary from your use of rhetorical questions to your use of the entire essay as the piece-by-piece unraveling of a mystery laid out in the first page of your report. Let us give a few more details of each. Rhetorical questions make the material more intriguing by momentarily stimulating the reader to wonder about some additional aspect of your group. For example, you might end a section that had described your group's philosophy about money by asking, "But what does this have to do with dieting?" The connection may seem befuddling, mysterious, or nebulous to the reader. Your next paragraph may then begin to weave the connections between these two seemingly disparate facets of their lives.

You might consider beginning your essay with a mystery. This can be done in two possible ways. You can open up an early paragraph with a rhetorical question that requires the rest of your essay to answer. For example, you might ask, "Why would a group of people cling desperately to ethnic traditions when it impedes them from economic opportunity?" or "Why do people give up a traditional life to live in celebate solitude?"

An alternate method for creating early mystery is to describe your own befuddlement or intrigue with a new word, concept, or group behavior. Then take the reader through your stepwise journey of discovering the answer. You may even consider adding some of your dead-end avenues of inquiry or your continuing misconceptions. David Lee's story of the !Kung and the Christmas Ox is a superb example of this.

Using Collage

Some ethnographers find it useful to employ the technique of collage when writing their report. This is an assembly of fragments or selections from diverse works to create a unified whole. This approach can yield a fuller, richer description of both the people being studied and the writer's fieldwork experience than a simple straightforward approach to writing the report; however, it is only one of many formats that can be used successfully.

The pages of your field notes and reflective journal contain a diversity of material with which to create a collage-type report. You may wish to select direct quotations, paraphrased dialogue, and pertinent portions of your reflective journal. Students may find that much of the final report has already been written on the pages of their field notes and reflective journal, and that by careful thought, selection, and arrangement of key portions they can create a coherent work that gives the reader a real sense of the writer's experience. We do not mean to minimize the final task of writing the report, however; the diverse hodgepodge of materials from both sources should be considered to be the raw materials for the final "distillation" process from which you make your descriptions and draw your conclusions. Excerpts from your field notes and journal can add color, meaning, and a sense of immediacy for your readers.

Other materials to consider for a collage-type report are poems, song lyrics, proverbs, or maxims. When this type of material originates within the culture you are studying, it may represent a shared understanding and, in a sense, allows the people to speak for themselves. This type of material is useful in both introducing and summing up important points or analyses within your report. In a study where your community has a distinct sense of ethnicity, use lyrics, poems, or proverbs that *belong* to the culture you are studying. To use material from your own culture might constitute an imposition of your own worldview on the other community. The exception to this rule would be a case where you are using the material to describe your personal experiences in the process of fieldwork.

One method of juxtapositioning material that is effective is to follow one piece of information with one of contrasting viewpoint. This can create a sarcastic or humorous response in the reader. Such a use of material is called irony. Why might you want to create irony? Perhaps you wish to contrast your findings with a media image or with the conclusions of another investigator. A student who was studying a rest home contrasted her findings with the photographs and descriptions contained in a promotional brochure. In these cases, authors are making statements through their irony—they are telling us that conditions may not be the way they have been depicted by others.

Using Informant Quotes

During your interviews with informants, you should have collected the most poignant and colorful communications in the form of direct quotes. Because the philosophy behind dialogical hermeneutic research dictates that the researcher allow the subjects to speak for themselves, you should consider these quotes to be some of your most "weighty" and credible material. A direct quote is a powerful tool in expressing a conclusion that you have drawn from your larger pool of data. Take care when selecting the quotes that the informant's identity is protected. You may need to edit the quote by altering or omitting specific information without changing the impact or meaning of the informant's words.

There may be times when you wish to relate for your readers an entire conversation. If you used a tape recorder during your interviews, you have the material before you, word-for-word. Dwyer used transcribed conversations in his final report, which gives the reader a real sense of being present during Dwyer's fieldwork. Some people can get direct quotes and complete conversations through note-taking. Conversations can also be reconstructed or paraphrased from your field notebook, but the reader should be made aware that the conversation presented to them is your recollection or paraphrased account of the actual conversation.

Ask the informants you are quoting for feedback during the first-draft stage of your writing. The research process is not necessarily over when the writing begins, and if your informant does not agree with the context in which you use his or her quote (i.e., to support a conclusion), then you need to further negotiate his or her meaning. Especially in the case of paraphrased conversations, look to your informants for validation of that section of your report.

Writing about Lived Experience

When writing about lived experience you are attempting to share with your reader the actual experience in all of its dimensions—physical, intellectual, emotional, and spiritual. To begin with, you need to allow the reader access to your five senses through the use of sensory detail. Most writers make good use of the senses of sight and sound, but neglect the other three; smell, taste, and touch. To capture, for example, the experience of participating in a Native American sweat lodge ceremony, an ethnographer would obviously fall short if he or she described only the setting and the music and speech. With the inclusion of concrete detail describing smells, tastes, and tactile sensations the picture is made fuller, though only on the physical level. The writer must also describe the emotions he or she experienced during the event, his or her thoughts, and any spiritual experience. Review your rough draft for terms that are vague and try to be as specific as possible using concrete terms that "show" rather than "tell" the experience to your reader—the "telling" comes in the analysis.

Painting Yourself into the Picture

One of the most rewarding aspects we have found as readers of hermeneutic ethnography is the opportunity to understand through description not only the community under study, but the ethnographer and his or her ethnographic "journey." Disclosure of the researcher's process of understanding is part of the theory of hermeneutic research; therefore, we encourage you to "paint yourself into the picture" when you write your final report. One student-ethnographer found in her study of Vietnam veterans little about her subjects that would not be considered common knowledge, but in her final report, she related her own powerful experience of motivation, self-discovery, and catharsis through the hermeneutic process of sharing another's understanding of reality. Many of her readers found their own confusion and mixed feelings concerning Vietnam veterans validated and dealt with in reading her intensely personal account. Although this particular ethnography was an exception—we *do* want to learn more about the group you are studying—it illustrates the value of including yourself and your personal fieldwork experience in your final paper. Karen McCarthy Brown had this to say about her book *Mama Lola*: "I chose to present myself as a character in the story, interacting with Alourdes. The challenge was to do this enough to reveal the way in which I relate to her without turning the book into a story about me."

Although you should not seek to produce an entirely humorous essay, the occasional addition of humor can enliven your account. The best type of humor to use is that which points to your own frailties. This could include descriptions of your misinterpretations of behaviors or statements of group members, your clumsy attempts to fit in with the group, or your informants' jokes about you. David Borshay Lee has included such episodes in "Eating Christmas in the Kalahari," keeping his descriptions short:

> "Fat?" /gau shot back, "You call that fat? This wreck is thin, sick, dead!" And he broke out laughing. So did everyone else. They rolled on the ground, paralyzed with laughter. Everybody laughed except me; I was thinking.

Barbara Gallatin Anderson also laughs at herself quite frequently in her book, *First Fieldwork*. The following is an example:

> Enthusiastic with my morning's productivity, I spread the map across the tabletop, imagining it completed and occupying a prominent place in a lovely, scholarly treatise that would electrify the anthropological world. Suddenly I was intrigued by a brown circle centrally located on the paper. I wondered what it was doing there and why it was growing ever larger even as I looked at it. Too late came the realization of what the pungent odor and crackling sound had already conveyed to a startled dining room and to my quick-witted waiter, who raced across the room, pitcher of water in hand. I had in my reverie, lowered the map onto one of the votive candle lamps that provided a decorous tone to the new "continental" dining room decor. As flames leaped from the map I could see the erect figures of restaurant guests looming about its edges, arms in the air, like stylized bodies in a cave painting. I clung hypnotically, riveted to the disappearing map. Then I felt a sharp slap to my wrist as a man forced from my hands the burning fragments. They fell to the white tablecloth, just as my rescuer and I felt the full impact of the waiter's pitcher of ice water upon us. The man was the chief pilot of the village, and by morning, news of the event had spread through the village as the little thatched community girded itself for winter with a pyromaniac.

Specific aspects of your personal fieldwork experience that you will want to consider incorporating into your final ethnography include: (1) personal history, (2) describing your feelings, (3) using dialogue, (4) describing challenges, (5) providing thick description, (6) presenting a sense of time and change, and (7) describing the process of fieldwork.

Personal History

You can give your reader insights into your worldview, your biases, and sensitivities, as well as your motivations when you include personal history. Your prior experiences, as they relate to the study, add not only human interest but provide your reader with additional tools with which to analyze your study. Here are examples from students:

My activism left when George went to Vietnam. I could no longer protest or be vocal about how I felt. I withdrew to my immediate family, but I still watched with sadness and with inner frustration all of the social upheaval and unrest about the war. I had not changed my opinions.

Growing up, I was fairly sheltered from ethnic prejudice, both by lack of exposure to minorities, and by attitudes communicated by significant people in my life: parents, teachers, and peers. We had a series of live-in babysitters—three sisters from Mexico who came, individually, to stay with us when my mother went back to work. They provided me with an exposure to Spanish at an early age and their presence was a thoroughly positive experience. The few blacks, Hispanics, and Asians in my schools were well liked, and, growing up in the sixties, I was exposed to racial strife only via television.

. . . I had given a lot of thought to the kind of juveniles these might be . . . I had thought a lot about my own teen years and how easily I could have slipped into a crack and found myself in an institution very much like this one (or more likely, a worse one in those days).

Describing Your Feelings

You give your reader the opportunity to share your fieldwork experience when you include the emotions you experienced during your study.

He granted me permission to do the study and reiterated what Jim had told me about the nature of the crimes committed by these young men. ". . . rape, murder, armed robbery . . . ," he said when I asked what kinds of crimes they had committed. It made me quite nervous. The comfort level slipped back a bit.

I became depressed and then felt guilty for being depressed. These Vets have lived with their feelings for at least twenty years. Where was I?—home safe, watching the war news during my evening meal, knowing pretty much what would happen tomorrow. They were in Vietnam wondering "if" there would be a tomorrow. I dug myself a hole of misery and crawled around in it trying to get a grip. I didn't want to go to school: everything seemed intertwined; everything seemed trivial compared to what I had heard.

Using Dialogue

The following excerpt of conversation from Kevin Dwyer's fieldwork illustrates the way in which dialogue can create a sense of immediacy for the reader as well as allow for deeper understanding.

K.D.: Formerly, had you talked of bringing his eldest daughter, Mehuba, here, for your son? No? Not at all? [I was responding to the Faqir's negative looks.]

FAQIR: No, no, no.

K.D.: I thought I had heard that?

FAQIR: Why would I want to bring Mehjuba here? Why?

K.D.: Before all this had happened.

FAQIR: No! You didn't hear that in this house. We never discussed such a thing. Fatima is the one who started the story about my bringing Nehjuba here. She told them, "Faquir asked me, 'I want Nehjuba for Mehdi.'" She started that.

K.D.: And you had said nothing? Had she said this so that perhaps you would change and want to bring her here?

FAQIR: Maybe, likely, probably.

K.D.: And now, where might this whole matter end up?

FAQIR: The matter will go where Our Owner wants it to.

K.D.: I mean, what are the different paths that it might take, according to your thinking?

FAQIR: We don't yet know where the Lord wants to take it, where he will take it.

K.D.: No, we don't know what will happen in the future.

FAQIR: Now, if there is agreement, fine. Otherwise it won't be a long time before I'll bring my daughter back here. That's all.

K.D.: When you saw them yesterday and when you spoke with them, did they seem agreeable or disagreeable?

FAQIR: Oh, my daughter's spirits were very low; she was doing nothing but crying.

K.D.: No, I didn't mean to ask that. Did you find that they were in good faith, or not?

FAQIR: You'll never find good faith there. Not on your life! Always good faith is lacking there. They say one thing and do another. Never is good faith present. Impossible! Not on your life! Not present in Fatima, in any case. Yet that 'Aisha, even though she's a tough one, she's all right.

K.D.: What do you mean, "even though she's a tough . . ."?

FAQIR: Even though, you know, she is shrewd, she's O.K., O.K. She doesn't hide things.

K.D.: You mean she speaks frankly?

FAQIR: Straightforwardly. And Bukhensha, he has his good faith.

K.D.: And when he first brought me here, did you know that their house was no good.

FAQIR: No. I didn't know Fatima hardly at all. And Mehjuba, I didn't know her at all.

K.D.: I still don't understand at all. You tell me this and I still don't . . .

FAQIR: I didn't know them well. I'd go there, you know, and when I'd go there, Fatima would make a fuss over me. And I said, "There is nothing wrong here." And Mehjuba, I didn't even know she was there. I thought there was just 'Aisha, and 'Aisha was very young then. And the other son who is always away, I don't know him. And the other one whom they say she bore in the wilds, I didn't know him then, and I still haven't met him.

Dwyer presents the give-and-take of interviewing; the negotiating.

Describing Challenges

You will have in-depth entries in your reflective journal describing the challenges that were presented in your study. Share your preconceptions and reformulation of understand with your readers.

> But Carla's spoken English is extremely limited, and as a result, she is isolated. At one point she referred to her home as a "prison" and herself as a "prisoner" . . . Through my fieldwork, Carla and I became good friends. What I at first took for contentment and commitment to her traditional role, I later discovered was resignation and depression. A dutiful Hispanic wife, she had followed her husband's desire to come here, and like others have told me, discovered the pain of intense loneliness.
>
> I sought intergenerational continuity, instead, I found great intergenerational variability due to the movement of many miners' sons out of the industry. The boom of the 1970s had attracted sons of farmers, merchants and teachers while miners' sons had been encouraged to move out of the area to obtain an education or skill. I had also noted that modern changes such as mass communication and mechanized transportation had apparently affected the more recent generations of residents who had grown up with the television and the automobile. They were less isolated and less unique than their predecessors.

Providing Thick Description

You may collect enough data in your short study to present a lengthy description of a feeling of your group, or a value, or a set of values, or their understanding of a phenomenon. Using adjectives, metaphors, quotes, applications, manifestations, and all aspects of variability within your group, you can provide information that surrounds your reader like a thick atmosphere.

> According to these insiders, force and exploitation were never issues. It seems that they attained a level of satisfaction in laboring which they valued. They were pragmatic in two senses. They saw the company as providing the necessary means to a livelihood—to living a comfortable life. At the same time, they chose to create a system of meaning—a source of satisfaction—within a structure provided by the company. There were pride, dignity, rules, traditions, and sanctions—all within a work situation framed by industry.
>
> There was pride, not only in physical ability, in providing for one's family, and in being a good worker, but in workmanship itself. The former mineworker told me:

> The older guys had pride in workmanship—setting a prop (timber to hold the roof up and to warn of possible cave-in) right and knowin' that it would hold the roof. They'd know where to pick the coal, pick it with the grain. They'd know how to sharpen the pick. It was like it was a craft—like making this tabletop, getting it smooth under your touch.

With the introduction of machine-loading, there was pride in crew production:

> I remember we had a competition in runnin' shuttle cars. We'd look for the chalk marks (on the frame of the shuttle car), at how far the shift before us got. Most of the time it was a pride that drove us . . . It wasn't a force from the boss—it came from the men themselves. I remember when I was a mineworker, the miner operator (continuous mining machine operator) was an older man. He'd yell at the buggy runner (shuttle car driver) for bein' so slow and for not getting off the shuttle car to help at the face to speed things up or to just help the crew.

There was dignity in providing just labor for an agreed upon wage. There was also a sense of dignity in discipline, skill, and endurance. My informant used the analogy of football:

> It's like the Penn State football team: Joe Paterno believes in hitting hard—no razzle, dazzle. You might lose 42 to 20, but you'd still have pride.

The rules included loyalty to the company, providing a just labor for an agreed upon wage, earning as much as one can, and providing as much as possible for one's family.

The traditions included being taken into the mines, apprenticeship, and indoctrination. I recalled a statement which my informant had made to me months earlier.

> I'd be there in the wash house soapin' up, and here'd be all these guys old enough to be my father or grandfather with fingers and tips of fingers missin', with their beer guts hangin' out. They'd growl: "So, kid you like to work in the fuckin' mine, eh?" Years later I found myself in the wash house growlin' to the younger guys: "So, kid you like to work in the fuckin' mine, eh?" That's when you know you made it.

The sanctions included knocking. I heard more stories of mineworkers knocking other mineworkers than stories of bosses knocking mineworkers. My informant told me: "You would embarrass them to help you because you were low rate." There was also the action of "dumping a buddy." My informant described it as it occurred in a mechanized mine:

> If you had a buddy who wasn't good, you tried to dump him. For example, if you were running shuttle cars with someone who was slow. (Two shuttle cars serviced one continuous miner. They alternated trips from the coal face to belts which took the coal from the mine. Roof bolters also worked in pairs and the continuous miner operator had a helper).

I recalled a former miner giving me an example from hand-loading days:

> The boss would give me an old man as a buddy. Those old men—they were worn out. All their sap was drained from years of hard work. We'd load a car, and the old man would want to stop for a drink of water. Then we'd work a little more, and he'd want to break for a pipe. I told him, "The trip's goin' to be comin' and we're goin' to lose a car." They would only drop you off as many empties as you had loaded cars. Finally, I told him to get out, and I worked by myself. I took the cars like I had a partner workin' with me.

There may have even been certain axioms involved in the work attitude. For example, I saw a sign above my informant's desk in his den. It read: "Good things come to he who waiteth as long as he who waiteth worketh like hell while he waiteth."

As in previous discussions with me, my informant took time to speak about the attitude of young miners who entered the mines in the late 1960s or 1970s. He described how they lacked the desire to work hard. If equipment broke down they often just sat around. It sounded to me as if work had lost meaning for them—as if work had become a painful process to endure. Without an appreciation for the traditions and satisfactions of the old work attitude their work life became aimless and meaningless. My informant pitied them.

> I still say that a lotta young guys were cheated. They thought that was the way it was supposed to be. They never learned what caused them to get to this time. They didn't know about hard times, hard work, the depression. All they knew was: "I can walk off the street and get one hundred dollars a day, and the union backs me. I don't have to work all that hard . . ." Today, if you can get *out* of doin' something—that's smart! (something to be proud of).

I recalled his saying in earlier interviews:

> They changed the rules so that you didn't need to have someone sign you in for a year as an apprentice. The company could hire as many as it wanted . . . These newer men just didn't understand. These guys were brought in when times were good—it was big bucks. Who knows, maybe some of them would have accepted the old ways if they would have had the chance to learn. In the old days you were indoctrinated to work at everything when you were in the mines. The newer fellahs were usually indoctrinated to one job—that's all. That would be their job description. It wasn't their fault. They came into the mines when times were good and never got the opportunity to gain from the experiences of the older miner.

He also told me:

> The work attitude was a handed down thing—a real individual need to do good.

Presenting a Sense of Time and Change

Your study will take months from inception to completion. Let your readers see how your understanding evolved over a period of time, and how the fieldwork experience itself changed during the course of the study. Here are two examples from student ethnographies.

> At the outset I was terribly nervous. I did not know what to expect. My biggest concern was that I would not be accepted and that the group would not open up to me . . . For the first several visits I would leave wondering if I was making any

headway at all. I did not begin to relax with the group until my third or fourth visit. I was beginning to get a sense that I was being honest with them.

When I grasped the idea of a process unfolding here, I realized that each immigrant woman I had interviewed seemed to be at a different place along that road to independence in direct relation to the number of years since immigration.

Describing the Process of Fieldwork

Sometimes the successes and failures of fieldwork present an understanding of the people. The process of carrying out the method then becomes part of the data. You should include interactions with informants that grew out of your attempts at analysis. The following is an example from Barry's research:

> When I began interviewing people, I expected the topics of danger and worry to be spoken about most often. What I found is that men frequently talked of the dangers lurking in the mine, of disasters and near disasters, and of their vigilance. It was as if they were celebrating their own survival within the atmosphere of potential catastrophe. Occasionally they would speak of their fears or worries, but most often men denied ever having them. Women seldom introduced the topic of danger or worry. It was only after several months of interviews that I began to ask questions directly on those topics. I found that when *I* introduced the topics women responded. Why had they held back talking to me of danger and worry? Why did they take my questions with such seriousness?

Another example comes from a student who studied spousal violence:

> My frustration continued. The professionals I called stated that they would call back, but no one did. My follow-up calls proved useless as well. No one was willing to talk to me. I began to think that perhaps the topic was too shameful or odious to discuss. Maybe that was why it remained so hidden. Maybe there was a massive cultural form of denial occurring. I was at a loss to explain how it was that so many people knew someone, but no one knew anyone who would talk to me.

> I began to suspect that those who tried to help victims or perpetrators of domestic violence might also be trying to protect them. I was frequently asked why I wanted to talk to these people. What was the purpose of inquiry? What was qualitative research? And how did I intend to use it? Once they were assured that I was trying to understand the complexities of domestic violence, they were eager to help. Still, they knew of no one who was willing to talk. The victims and perpetrators remained obscure.

We hope that these examples and suggestions aid you in putting together your ethnographic essay. You may find that you have more data and more ideas than you had realized.

"Building a Case": Problems in Writing Ethnography

One of the traps that you must avoid in writing your ethnograhic essay is "case building." In English Composition classes students are taught how to build a convincing case for their point of view in their expository writing. In carrying this out the students emphasize arguments and evidence supportive of their position while refuting counterarguments and dismissing counterevidence. This can be dangerous in ethnographic writing because it can reduce the number of voices heard and the variation in response. Seldom will all members of a group present one line of thinking or feeling about topics of interest to them. What you should expect is a rich diversity of opinions and experiences, although one or more may dominate. By merely giving your readers a convincing portrayal of the dominant (or one of the dominant) pictures you may be misleading the reader into thinking that one monolithic worldview exists for the group.

Case building can become even more deceptive if one is only calling on data to support a description while ignoring any discrepant responses. Lawyers are trained to use this ploy. By neglecting to tell the judge and jury of any incriminating evidence involving his or her client, the lawyer is presenting a distorted, one-sided view of the client. Because it makes no attempt to explain the counterevidence, this is more deceptive than the expository writing mentioned above. You may find yourself tempted to present a consistent picture by ignoring a few pieces of data which "flaw" the consistency. Try to resist this trap. The nature of your understanding of your group should be one in which you see all the nuances of the group. Think of your description as a multifaceted gemstone, rather than a flat sliver of mica.

Exercises

9.1 Think of possible sources you might use to form a collage of information for your study. What information could be presented from each?

9.2 Using plots of movies, plays, and books as well as your own life experiences, news items, and fieldwork, list ten examples of irony.

9.3 Choose the three most intriguing, enlightening, or powerful quotes from your interviews. How do these relate to your overall analysis of the data?

PART III

ADVANCED CONSIDERATIONS

Chapter 10

USING LIVED EXPERIENCE

. . . novel ways of moving, talking, and interacting contribute to a visceral appreciation of the forces that occasion those actions.
—Robert R. Desjarlais

. . . knowledge is not purely cognitive. It is also the product of our emotional sensibilities and affinities.
—Dorinne K. Kondo

This chapter involves less urgent issues in learning how to do ethnography. Because of this, we recommend rereading the first nine chapters before tackling this information. This is particularly true if you are in the midst of carrying out a short fieldwork project.

We will begin by exploring some theoretical aspects of the subject of lived experience, and then we will apply these principles to the process of fieldwork, offering advice as well as description.

We ethnographers bring to our analysis our past experiences as well as those that will occur during the field study. To what extent can we use these experiences—as remembered in thoughts, bodily feelings, and emotions? Authors such as Bourdieu, Kondo, and Desjarlais have suggested that there are ways of knowing that go beyond the cognitive, that is, rational. We will refer to these as sensibilities. As the body experiences the world is it conditioned by culture to make a certain sense of the world?

BODILY ORIENTATIONS AND SENSATIONS

According to this point of view, there are tacit body orientations that teach cultural members what it is to be themselves. This can include a way of walking, a way of bowing in the presence of authority, a manner of squatting to smoke a cigarette, dance postures in ceremonial rituals, or a pious posture in church. This form of experience contributes to a "gut level" or visceral appreciation of the forces that contribute to the culturally created body orientation.

Other sensibilities can lead to this visceral appreciation: gestures (both made and perceived), odors, sound qualities, tastes, and tactile sensations. Thus, the hand clenched into a fist and held high in defiance, the smell of incense at religious services, the sound of ritual wailing at a funerary service, the taste of beer and pizza, the feel of vibrations from a drum during a shamanic curing ritual, or the feel of a pick handle in one's hands all contribute to bodily sensibilities and are culturally mediated. Bourdieu has suggested that such sensibilities contribute to one's understanding and appreciation of one's class and, as such, aid in preventing a person from advancing outside that class.

These sensibilities involve the embodying of cultural practices, of participating fully and effortlessly in the string of moments that constitute life in any given society. This participation shapes members' understanding of their values, tastes, and movements.

Assuming all of this is true, it becomes the anthropologist's task to give sense to the reader of what it feels like for a native to live in his or her culture. The approach that the ethnographer will take to accomplish this may be phenomenological and/or interpretive. The phenomenological approach, on the one hand, assumes that the ethnographer can feel in his or her body the experiences of daily life in the culture of study, that he or she can feel what the natives feel. In some cases this assumption seems valid to us; for example, taking up competitive bodybuilding during one's study of competitive bodybuilders would seem to give the investigator a good sense of their sensibilities.

On the other hand, many experiences are culturally mediated and, as such, require long-term enculturation, perhaps even childrearing experiences, for proper sensibility. So, what a !Kung bushman once experienced as a participant in trance dance ceremonies would not likely match what an outsider would have experienced. The !Kung experience an enhanced state of consciousness called *kia* that is a painful and feared prerequisite to healing. Activated *num* (energy) is said to boil fiercely in the person, causing the base of the spine to tingle and making thoughts turn to nothing in the dancer's head. The intense emotional state of *kia* allows the dancer to see everything, to see what is troubling everybody, to contact the spirit realm, and to see inside people's bodies. The !Kung learn to control the boiling energy in order to apply it to healing.

More to the point, Desjarlais was told during his study of a Yolmo shaman, that his novice experiences in trance were meaningless. Desjarlais, thus came to the conclusion that he had to learn some of the basic tenets of Yolmo experience, ways of the body and interacting with others, that might enable him to be a proper shaman.

We feel that these experiences of cultural immersion are useful for hermeneutic study regardless of their likely mismatch with native sensibilities. Often our experiences can shift our epistemology and provide a first step to empathy with informants. By an epistemic shift, we are referring to a shift from listening and recording what the native feels to actually feeling what he or she feels. In an earlier chapter we used the metaphor of a plant growing in soil to describe the process of empathy, saying that empathy grows from our ground(ing) in experience. So, the richer the ground of our experience, the more robust the growth of our understanding. Another way of thinking about this process is to compare it with a child's learning process. Parents often say: "He had to learn the hard way; he wouldn't listen to what I said." This can refer to two levels of understanding: the purely cognitive and the visceral. Sometimes a gut-level understanding of a situation through lived experience is necessary. This represents an epistemic shift. Good examples of such an epistemic shift have occurred for anthropologists such as Edith Turner and Michael Harner. Each of them have experienced supernatural phenomena during spiritual ritual that facilitates their visceral understanding of native spirituality (especially shamanism).

Edith Turner experienced a vision of objects that she was unable to identify while in a shamamic trance state. Four months later when she was carrying out fieldwork with Eskimos, she saw in her ordinary state of consciousness, the same objects. They were the internal organs of a seal. In another situation, she experienced seeing a large gray blob of something like plasma emerge from a sick woman's back during her participation in a Ndembu curing ceremony. Michael Harner experienced extensive visions in shamanic states of consciousness during fieldwork with the Jivaro and the Conibo. These are useful for the ethnographer because he or she can articulate his or her sensibilities to the native for comment, stimulating both conversation and reflection by the group member.

In other words, these provide a means for improving the use of the dialogical hermeneutic method. When the ethnographer chooses to describe his or her own experiences in the daily life or rituals of another culture, without native comment, problems arise. There will be a tendency to be preconditioned by his or her own cultural practices and previously learned metaphors that will distort what the investigator experiences and reports. This will include subcultures that you might investigate in your short initiation into fieldwork. For example, Barry ventured into a modern coal mine where he heard, smelled, felt internally, and felt tactilely what it was like to exist in this environment and "culture." Yet, these were not likely the sensibilities of the oldest generation of miners who had seen their fathers come home blackened every day, who had been taken into the mine at age sixteen (or earlier), and taught by their fathers how to interpret sounds, sights, and feelings, and who had spent fifty years of their lives in that environment, with fellow workers. The ethnographer needs to reflect on his or her own propensity to fantasize or romanticize another's existence based on this sort of "lived experience."

Emotional Sensibilities and Affinities

We briefly mentioned in chapter 8 the concept of dissolution of self in the process of cultural immersion. Kondo and Crapanzano include as a part of this process the emotional sensibilities and affinities that arise in the interpersonal exchanges with cultural members. It is this process, occurring while one is isolated from one's own culture, that causes one to lose one's old self and that catalyzes the constructing of a new self. Can this process of dissolution lead to more experiential and affective modes of knowing? Because the cultural members are enticing the investigator into behaviors and feelings by means of their "normal" ways of feeling, thinking, and behaving, the ethnographer may be feeling what some other cultural members would feel under similar circumstances. Of course, this varies with situations and personalities. Because transference and projection can become a part of this complicated phenomenon, it is difficult to say when the ethnographer is appropriately interpreting the behaviors, intentions, thoughts, and feelings of those with whom they are interacting. We described the process of transference and projection in chapter 6.

We feel that this lived experience can be one in which culturally shaped transferences are felt by the ethnographer, leading to insights about how group members understand and interact with one another. When dissolution and reconstitution of self occurs, an actual collusion may occur because the ethnographer and the group members intuitively understand how to act and react, based on the feelings that are generated. Kondo's situation makes this clear. As a Japanese American studying in Japan, she looked and, in some ways, felt Japanese. She made a concerted effort to conform to what she thought her informants' expectations of a daughter might be. Her behaviors seemed to please her informants as well as satisfy their sense of who she was. A reinforcement thus took place as she sought to continue the warm feelings of acceptance by conforming more closely to their expectations and as they assumed that she was acting autonomously and "naturally." One way to view this collusion is in terms of an ever-tightening relationship. We have illustrated this in Figure 10.1.

Indeed, Kondo felt increasingly under their power. In its use of the desire to please, this process resembles childhood encultura-

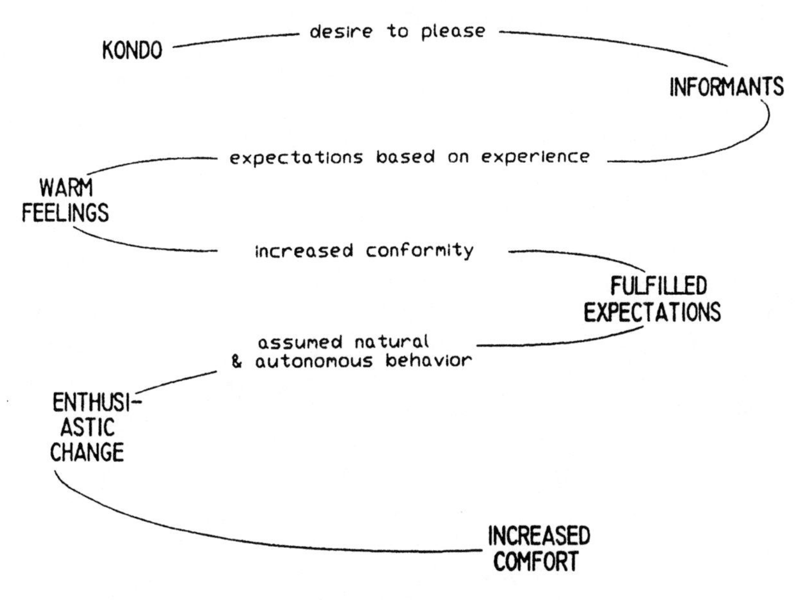

FIGURE 10.1
Collusion Between Kondo (Ethnographer) and Her Informants

tion (at least in some cultures). Gerber has suggested that for Samoans the desire to please is used to teach the child which feelings are appropriate for various situations. Gerber then described how she observed socially beneficial behaviors to follow from these enculturated feelings. Was Kondo beginning to feel culturally appropriate feelings via this enculturation process? In her own words: "At its most extreme point there was a total identification with Otherness, where the identity I had known in another context simply collapsed."

If the informants have the power to shape and control the behavior, feelings, and identity of the ethnographer, perhaps analysis of the lived experiences of the ethnographer can tell much about the group members' culturally shaped expectations and motivations. As was the case with bodily sensations, we feel that an understanding of these expectations and motivations need to be negotiated through dialogue with informants. The ethnographer's interpretation of his or her lived experience within the group of study alone is not enough to appropriately describe the culture being studied.

There are two distinctly different situations in which an ethnographer might apply lived experience: traditional studies of a culture different from one's own and studies of one's own culture. We will describe how phenomenology pertains to each situation and give some instructions for its best use in each ethnographic situation.

Studying One's Own Culture

This process has been referred to by the terms: native ethnography, indigenous ethnography, auto-ethnography, and insider research. Although the same principles of dialogical hermeneutics hold for insider research as for traditional studies, the process may prove to be more difficult. In fact, dialogical studies of one's own group may be impossible for the uninitiated ethnographer. For this reason we *do not recommend* such studies for a course in field methods. Although most of you will be working in American culture, we suggest your choosing a subculture with which you are unfamiliar. In what follows we will be addressing our instructions of method to students who already have experienced a fieldwork project.

There are both advantages and disadvantages to doing insider research. Among the positive features are the shortened time of entry into the group since one is already accepted and knows many informants, the immediate recognition of important group issues, the precondition of trust and openness with informants, the cooperation by group members out of desire to enhance the career of one of their own, a common understanding of nonverbal cues, the use of one's past lived experience as data, and the use of one's ongoing lived experience as data.

Disadvantages include the possibility that the group may not consider the ethnographer to be a member, the increased likelihood of projection and reductionism, problems maintaining confidentiality, and difficulties in recognizing challenges to one's understanding. The latter is especially troublesome because there is no exotic quality to behaviors and explanations that you will experience. Therefore, there will be less head-scratching confusion over new data.

Some investigators have been surprised by how quickly the advantages dissolve once one announces his or her decision to study the group. For example, trust may quickly turn to suspicion because informants feel vulnerable to the spread of gossip. Informants may decline to participate because they do not wish to jeopardize their friendship with the investigator. Recognition of group issues may in some instances mean that the investigator lacks an intriguing approach to questions. Likewise, the fact that one may already be defined in relationships may mean a lack of the freshness and/or tension that generates meaningful data. Many informants may end up resenting what they perceive as exploiting the group for one's own gain. Also, nonverbal cues, because they are understood, do not lead to confrontation and challenge. These nonverbal cues may be what appears intriguingly different about the group to an outsider.

Under circumstances such as these, the only unique advantage to insider research becomes one's appropriate use of past and ongoing lived experience. However, this requires a refined ability of reflexion.

In doing insider studies it is especially important for you to make early entries into your reflective journal. You will need to recall your past lived experiences, particularly those events, traditions, feelings, and sensibilities that you think make you a part of the group you are studying. In effect, you are recording notes of yourself as a key informant. You will also want to ask yourself to tie those sensibilities of which you are aware to group values.

In terms of biases, you will have a different objective from those doing outsider research. You need to be able to distinguish between culturally constructed (i.e., insider) preconceptions and your idiosyncratic (i.e., private) biases. This will be your major reflexive task. As a part of this responsibility you must be vigilant in your search for variability within the group. Yours may not be the only experiences, opinion, and understandings represented.

Since your challenges will be more difficult to discern, you should count on classmates and your adviser to be sensitive to cultural differences. Not only may they detect when your opinion and understanding are idiosyncratic, but they can help to discern when group values and understanding are uniquely different from the mainstream culture. This can often be difficult for an insider.

You will also need to take special care to not load your interview questions. Try to get the informant to do most of the talking, especially early in the interview. At the very end of the interview ask them to comment on your experiences. Depending on the disposition of the informant, he or she may not feel comfortable in disagreeing with you. There is the dangerous tendency for interviews to become friendship-seeking as you both note the similarities in your experiences. In some ways the encounter could resemble a scenario in which you are attending a wedding reception and happen upon someone from your hometown. There can be excitement in getting to know someone who you do not know and who has experienced some of the same conditions.

You will also need to be vigilant about ensuring that all voices are heard. In groups whose membership counts in the thousands and is regionally scattered, there may be many more voices than you have experienced prior to the field study; yet it is difficult to rid yourself of stereotypes that you have already created. Of course, this is less of a concern in small, regionally closed groups such as a local volunteer organization. However, one should never assume uniformity.

Formal methods of analysis, such as those described in chapter 4, may work particularly well for insider research. Because there may be a preexisting trust and familiarity with some group members, they may cooperate readily in more delving types of analyses. This type of strategy is also less likely to produce the condition of leading the informant, although you will need to be careful not to use leading questions in the construction of your protocol.

Do not be timid about taking advantage of your position in selecting key informants and fieldwork facilitators. Your prior contacts may prove to give you the most valuable information in depth and breadth. As long as you follow the precautions that we have suggested you should not feel guilty about the facility that these contacts provide.

Insider research presents an exceptional opportunity to share data with informants. This is particularly true if you have been a participating member in a group of twenty or fewer members. Should you enlist the cooperation of such members, you need only to worry about possible face-saving tactics by members as they make corrections in your notes. You may find that group members may be more sensitive to their individual and group images when seen in new data than they would have been in reading only the final report.

Be alert for culturally shaped transference. This is more likely in groups in which members have been enculturated at an early age, that is, an ethnic neighborhood. Do you get feelings based on the group members' moods, their timing of statements, expectations when they are ambiguously stated? Do you feel that group members are trying to manipulate your behaviors by appealing to your feelings? Answering yes to any of these could indicate transference. Reflecting more deeply on these instances may yield information that has not been directly spoken.

Visceral Feelings about the Cultural Other

To obtain visceral knowledge, you need to pay attention to what your body and sensations are telling you. Make certain that you record in your notebook any new sounds, odors, body feelings, or tastes. Those that are not new may also be important if they occur when you might not expect them. Try to assume postures, positions, and movements of informants. In this regard remind yourself of how important it is to sit in class and take notes in order to get the feel of what it is like to be a student.

A student who studied police officers and a student who studied volunteer firemen both experienced traveling with informants as they went "on call." Both students reported experiencing an "adrenaline rush," which they felt helped them understand their informants' experiences at a gut level. Both of the student ethnographers then asked their informants if they experience similar feelings. Another example of experiential knowledge of the other occurred when a female student, studying exotic dancers, visited the bar in which the dancers worked. As a young female, she experienced behaviors of male patrons that brought feelings to her that she could then later use in interviewing her informants. For example, as she made her course toward the ladies' room she experienced hearing males shout suggestive remarks to her behind her back. Feeling offended by these remarks and the way in which they were delivered, she wondered if the dancers commonly received such treatment, and if so, how they felt and how they reacted to it.

Feelings also arise through the stimulation of culturally shaped transference. Therefore, it is important to note in your journal those occasions when things feel "strange" between you and an informant. If an informant feels offended, betrayed, or treated unjustly, or if you feel any of these ways about one of your informants, it may indicate misinterpretation or mismatch of transference based on differences in cultural expectations or interpretations of behaviors.

Keep track also of those instances when you are seeking to please informants. What behaviors and/or feelings do you note in yourself? Do you feel as if the informant(s) are controlling you, sculpting your behavior and sensibilities to meet their cultural expectations?

Remember that, for the dialogical hermeneutic method, all of your instances of experienced sensibilities require feedback from informants to ensure proper interpretation. For the textual hermeneutic model, no such feedback is necessary. The only requirement is that the ethnographer interpret his or her feelings in a manner that ties in coherently with the description he or she is advancing for the study group. In this respect, it is more phenomenological than the dialogical hermeneutic model.

When research is based on lived experience you should write your report in such a way as to give readers an appreciation for the sensibilities of group members. By this, we mean that you should try to elicit a visceral understanding in the reader. This would be true regardless of the hermeneutic model being employed and regardless of whether it is insider or outsider research. The following are some examples of how this might be accomplished.

Writing about Lived Experience

When writing an ethnographic essay involving lived experience, the ethnographer should try to achieve two ends: to show how his or her experienced feelings relate to those of cultural members and to elicit feelings in the reader similar to those believed to be experienced by cultural members. You can best achieve this by extensive use of description. The following excerpts will give you some idea of how this is achieved.

This excerpt comes from Grimes's book on ritual:

> Breathing in *zazen* is breathing, period. Breathing also has a meaning, though intellectually contemplating this meaning is not part of *zazen*. As a ritualization process, breathing expresses how I flow from connectedness and symbiosis to isolation and solitude.... Breathing, we might say, is "selfing." It is how we flow into being without solidifying into selves, egos, souls, or other forms of clinging.... Mindful breathing, despite its being done repeatedly, is a gesture of dehabituation. It is a way of emptying and forming.

A student wrote this about her experiences in a bar in which she was studying exotic dancers:

> As I, myself, discovered, the customers are sometimes a drawback. During one of my visits to the bar, I was walking back to use the rest room. I passed by a group of men that would not look me in the eye, only to hear lewd and obscene comments about me as I was walking away. It scared me because it made me feel vulnerable and weak. The dancers seemed hardened to this conduct, but they also said that it was one of their biggest complaints about the job.

Colin Turnbull wrote the following description in *The Forest People*:

> For a month I sat every evening at the kumamolimo; listening, watching, and feeling—above all, feeling. If I still had little idea of what was going on, at least I felt that air of importance and expectancy. Every evening, when the women shut themselves up, pretending that they were afraid to see "the animal of the forest"; every evening, when the men gathered around the fire, pretending that they thought that the women thought the drainpipes were animals; every evening, when the trumpet drainpipes imitated leopards and elephants and buffalos—every evening, when all this make-believe was going on, I felt that

something very real and great was going on beneath it, something that everyone else took for granted, and about which I was ignorant.

It was as though the songs which lured the "animal" to the fireside also invoked some other kind of presence. As the evenings wore on toward morning, the songs got more and more serious, and the atmosphere not exactly tense but charged with an emotion powerful enough to send the dancers swirling through the molimo fire as though its flames and red-hot coals held no heat, as though the glowing embers were cold ashes. Yet there was nothing fanatic or frenzied about their action in dancing through the fire. Then there was always that point when the "animal" left the camp and returned to the forest, taking the presence with it. I could feel it departing as the mellow, wistful voice of the molimo got farther and farther away.

In *Thunder Rides a Black Horse,* Claire Farrer wrote:

> And, again, I was amazed at how I had learned not to hear that which did not concern me when in a tepee. I do not know when or how this occurred; I only remember being surprised one day when I realized I no longer had to concentrate on not attending to things that were not my business and no longer even heard them. Usually, at home, I awaken at every little noise; but when I am sleeping in a tepee, someone can rekindle a fire, handle a grate, put a bucket on it, bring in coffee, and do who knows what all else without either my ears or nose being aware.

Finally, we present two excerpts from Michael Harner's *The Way of the Shaman,* where he says the following about his experiences with shamanistic trance:

> I became conscious, too, of the most beautiful singing I have ever heard in my life, high-pitched and ethereal, emanating from myriad voices on board the galley. As I looked more closely at the deck, I could make out large numbers of people with the heads of blue jays and the bodies of humans, not unlike the bird-headed gods of ancient Egyptian tomb paintings. At the same time, some energy-essence began to float from my chest up into the boat. Although I believed myself to

> be an atheist, I was completely certain that I was dying and that the bird-headed people had come to take my soul away on the boat. While the soul-flow continued from my chest, I was aware that the extremities of my body were growing numb.
>
> Starting with my arms and legs, my body slowly began to feel like it was turning to solid concrete. I could not move or speak. Gradually, as the numbness closed in on my chest, toward my heart, I tried to get my mouth to ask for help, to ask the Indians for an antidote. Try as I might, however, I could not marshal my abilities sufficiently to make a word. Simultaneously, my abdomen seemed to be turning to stone, and I had to make a tremendous effort to keep my heart beating. I began to call my heart my friend, my dearest friend of all, to talk to it, to encourage it to beat with all the power remaining at my command.

and:

> I went to his hut, taking my notebook with me, and described my visions to him segment by segment. At first I told him only the highlights; thus, when I came to the dragon-like creatures, I skipped their arrival from space and only said, "There were these giant black animals, something like great bats, longer than the length of this house, who said that they were the true masters of the world." There is no word for dragon in Conibo, so "giant bat" was the closest I could come to describe what I had seen.
>
> He stared up toward me with his sightless eyes, and said with a grin, "Oh, they're always saying that. But they are only the Masters of Outer Darkness."
>
> He waved his hand casually toward the sky. I felt a chill along the lower part of my spine, for I had not yet told him that I had seen them, in my trance, coming from outer space.
>
> I was stunned. What I had experienced was already familiar to this barefoot, blind shaman, known to him from his own explorations of the same hidden world into which I had ventured.

These are but short excerpts in what are pages and chapters of description. The more detailed and extensive your descriptions of the feelings and consequences of lived experience, the better.

EXERCISES

10.1 Think about your childhood experiences and what it is like to "be home." What sensibilities of this culture can you describe? Think of special odors, sounds, tastes, tactile sensations, postures. They need not be pleasant sensations. Write a paragraph or two about these sensibilities.

10.2 Spend a short time in a "foreign culture." This could be a walk through Chinatown, attending services in a new church, doing volunteer work at a soup kitchen, attending a festival, or going to a small-town diner. What new sensations did you experience? Write a paragraph or two describing these sensibilities.

10.3 Create a scenario in which you will act out a role with another person. You will play yourself. Write clearly the *behavior* that your partner should display. You should not explain the motivation behind the behavior. Act out the scene. Have your partner write down the feeling evoked by this scenario. Was the knowledge he or she obtained accurate?

Chapter 11

ORAL HISTORY

Because history is experienced in common, the narratives . . . reveal a great deal about the effect particular historical forces had on family, ethnic and local histories.

—*Carl Oblinger*

We have decided to include a separate chapter on oral history because those students specifically interested in this area will find that there are some theoretical and technical issues that they should consider. We will present each theoretical issue along with some practical suggestions on how to treat it. Although we have referred to several publications in writing this chapter, we have found Oblinger's book: *Interviewing the People of Pennsylvania* to be the most beneficial. You may wish to read it.

Those of you who are oral historians are often pressed harder than other class members to define "truth" to your readers. You need to answer the question of whose perspective, that is, whose truth, is being presented. Is it the people's perspective? the writer's perspective? or are the events and interpretations objective? Since you will be presenting data from archival sources such as newspaper articles, you are likely to be presenting a perspective from the time of past events as well as one from the memories of contemporary informants.

Ideal versus Real

In some cases the archival information can be used to provide the context for informants' reflections on the past. For example, a study of people's feelings about the unionizing efforts in the coalfields in the 1930s need to be understood in the context of recorded events such as prior mine closings, union contracts, national politics, economic conditions, and union leaders. Newspaper articles and union correspondence could provide information for such a context.

Because, at times, archival information and people's memories do not match, you may have to find a way of explaining such discrepencies. First, let us say that these may represent hermeneutic "challenges" to your understanding as an investigator. While the logical process for your resolving such a challenge would be to ask informants about information that disagrees with their assessment, such a step must be carried out without threatening your fieldwork relationships. Consider the possibility that it will sound as if you are accusing them of faulty or prejudiced memory to say that you read something contrary to their account. One solution to this quandary is to try phrasing your question with doubt about the written material: "I wonder if the news reporter was ill-informed or misinformed?" In any case, try to remain humble and trusting in your approach to asking about the discrepencies.

Some oral historians use the discrepency between archival and oral accounts to present conflict to the reader. Often this is done in the mode of an "ideal versus real" framework. The question then becomes: Which is the ideal and which the real world? Let us explain. Some investigators might find that informants reflect back to the ideals of the time and selectively forget that there were many exceptions to that ideal. The archival accounts might point out this selectivity. Conversely, archival information may reflect past leaders' ideals or the ideals of one particular class while today's informants may point out what real conditions were like.

Many ethnographers choose to point out the discrepency and allow the reader to deal with the epistemological challenge of sorting out real from ideal. This route is closest to the philosophy of hermeneutics. In Barry's book about coal-mining families he first interpreted men's actions and attitudes about mine mechanization in terms of owning-class exploitation of workers. He then presented an opposing point of view offered by workers. Because it came last, the workers' point of view seems to hold more weight, but both perspectives are presented.

Some analysts such as Bodnar and Grele appear suspicious of the memories of informants. They feel that memories can be heavily influenced by factors such as the values of mass society, by structures of power and social discourse, by current conditions, and/or by personalizing of the past. We will say a few words about each of these.

Over the years the values and images of mass society have pervaded the subcultures throughout the United States. Systems such as mass media, mass transportation, and higher education have allowed the mainstream ideology to touch even the most isolated enclaves. Thus, an informant from Appalachia, who may not have been greatly affected by mass society in the 1930s, is thinking back while deeply immersed in today's mass society. Will this affect his or her memories?

There are other ways in which present conditions could conceivably shape memories. An example would be retired miners who now live comfortably on pension, social security, and black lung payments, thinking about how the future looked to them in the lean years of the 1930s. Conversely, laid-off railway workers, now living less meaningful lives, may not remember the satisfaction of their past existence, *or* might overly value it.

The power structure of the historical epoch of the time may have influenced people's thinking, and thus their current memories. If a company affected worker's thinking with propaganda or limited such factors as the style of management, the ethnic makeup of the work force or the social interaction among workers, then people thinking back on those times might be unable to see the "big picture" of what was going on.

Some people tend to personalize the past. By this we mean that they tend to see themselves as independent of the values and actions of a group or of power structures—as if all of what happened in their lives was unique to them and, to a certain extent, under their control. Again, they miss the "big picture" of social forces that were involved and of groups or classes of people who experienced similar forces and phenomena.

In comparing the ideal and real, the ethnographer is actually calling into question one version of "the truth." Thus, this process involves an epistemological issue. Is the "objective" truth purported by scholars or news writers questionable in light of informants' intersubjective truth, or is informants' intersubjective truth questionable in the light of the "objective" truth of archival data? According to the epistemological stance of dialogical hermeneutics presented in chapters 1 and 2, the intersubjective truth should always be sought and presented, never dismissed, even if it is contrasted with conclusions drawn from archival data.

Choosing Informants

To a certain extent, the process of recording oral history requires some different concerns in the selection of informants. A good informant should exhibit qualities of good memory, enjoyment of the process of talking about the past, self-confidence in his or her narration, and detailed knowledge about events. It is difficult to say why a person gains a detailed knowledge about past events. Sometimes their profession, or the profession of their spouse or parent, requires them to be aware of political events and policies of structural changes, or of family genealogies. In other cases, the person is simply a competent observer of the social scene.

Factors to keep in mind with regard to knowledge include the number of years the person lived in the area, whether he or she has been an accepted member of the population being discussed, and the variety of experiences the narrator can call on to interpret social structures, changes, and interactions. Remember that the informant should be an eyewitness to the things he or she describes. Second- or thirdhand reports are very difficult to assess. A notable exception would be stories that are a part of a passed-down oral tradition.

Interviewing Strategies

The nature of your interviewing will depend on the nature of the group you are studying. While there are modes of variation among groups, one major distinction is whether the group includes people of all ages, childhood enculturation, and geographical place. A neighborhood or a village would qualify as such a subculture. In contrast, a club, a profession or job occupation (e.g., dock workers), a company, or an agency (e.g., a volunteer fire company) would be less life-encompassing and intergenerational. We will speak about this distinction as we talk about interviewing.

Whether studying a residential area or an organization, you should try to determine the member's impressions of the group's physical landscape. For a town or neighborhood, this includes important geographical and climatological information: surrounding communities, plant life, topography, bodies of water, parks, pollution, cloud cover, streets, houses, and shopping areas. For organizations, it will mostly include the building(s) in which the organization functions or regularly meets. What does the physical landscape contribute to people's behaviors and understandings?

Memories may have a strong component that is direct, tactile, and concrete. Asking informants about smells, sounds, or tastes of the past may bring to mind other memories associated with these. Many remembered experiences are first reexperienced as emotional. Barry found that informants, reflecting back to a time over sixty years past, reconciled strong feelings they had for strikebreakers and company police during the 1927 coal strike. We recommend building on both emotional and concrete memories, expanding outward to more historically detailed memories.

Our readings in oral history methods lead us to suggest that changes occurring over time are an essential element to most studies. You can obtain this perspective of change by requesting it from informants or by contrasting accounts that were presented with regard to specific eras of the group being studied, perhaps by different-aged informants. What we mean is that informants might tell you, "This is the change that we experienced," or informants of different ages (and therefore eras) might say, "This is the way things were," and you, as analyst, will note the change in experiences over generations. Should you choose the latter strategy, try to find older informants to critique or corroborate your analysis. They *may* present a hermeneutic "challenge" to your interpretation.

Many older informants will talk about themselves, possibly as a way to understand the meaning and importance of their lives. The descriptive data from an informant's life story can be used as a means for developing questions about social change and perceived problems associated with it. For example, an informant might talk about losing a job, going back to college, or experimenting with drugs. How does he or she view these life events in the "big picture" of social change? How have these changes affected other members of his or her group or community?

Some things to keep in mind about memories is that details are often associated with seemingly unrelated special events in people's lives. These might include disasters like the Mississippi River flood of 1993 or the year of the devastating drought, with national events such as a presidential election, with locally significant events such as the year the shopping mall was built or the year that a landmark restaurant burned down, or with personal events such as a pregnancy, a birth, a death, a serious illness, or someone's graduation.

You will benefit from keeping track of each informant's "time markers" so that you can refer back to them if necessary. For example, you might ask, "Was that before or after your father's death?" You might also suggest some time markers to informants if they do not seem to be using them. Sometimes markers of other informants may work as suggestions.

As an investigator, you are likely to benefit from asking to borrow personal materials such as photo albums, scrap books, diaries, newspaper and magazine clippings, and mementos such as awards, postcards, printed programs, posters, and fliers. There is a possible threefold reward here: the material itself may prove to have historically relevant data, it may stimulate the informant's memory, and it may provide you with questions to pursue in future interviews, particularly with new informants.

Five areas of people's social lives seem to be of greatest importance: family, work, education, community, and religion. In studying the oral history of a subculture such as a town or neighborhood, you should keep these topics in mind. Broad topics for organizations and occupations can include group goals, networks, internal conflicts, and relations with outside organizations.

Oblinger has suggested that oral historians investigating small towns focus on the social structure of the community. This seems to be an important direction in the study of any group. You could directly question informants about the social structure and social relations in their groups. For communities, this could include asking what group dominated the town or neighborhood or provided a focus for community activities. Possible answers are: churches, political bosses, clubs, or industry. For any group, you could ask if there were differences in the prestige or power of group members or cliques. Even clubs and work situations have leaders. You might ask, "Who were past leaders?" "What style did they display?" and "How did they become leaders?"

For villages, Oblinger recommended identifying corporate groups. These are the groups that carry the culture of any village. Examples would include a lineage, a powerful secret society, or a political party.

He suggested asking informants to trace corporate groups backward as well as forward in time. He also presented the notion of asking informants about community celebrations and special days since these are often used to reinforce the value to communities of a certain ideology (i.e., values, attitudes, and philosophy).

Relationships within a group are important. For a residential group this could involve family relations. It is important for you to find out which family members have remained in the community before exploring the nature of family relations. Relationships outside the family could include: customer-proprietor, artisan-client, professional-client, or clergy-congregation. For agencies or clubs, relationships could include: supervisor-worker, officers-members, or initiates-long-standing members.

Other avenues for broad questions could be past events or processes. We described event analysis and process analysis in chapter 7. You may wish to review that material before planning your interviews.

Remember that gathering data through oral history involves a dialogical process. If you conduct more than one interview with each informant you are likely to be rewarded by the reflection and stimulation processes in remembering. Also, *you* will be thinking about the past interview, looking for areas in which you would like extra details or clarification.

Exercises

11.1 Spend five or ten minutes thinking about time markers that you use to determine when things occurred in the past. Write these down and classify them as national, local, or personal. Pair up with a classmate and discuss each other's markers. Following the discussion compare and contrast each other's markers.

11.2 Write a short essay in which you describe the personality and physical landscape of your current neighborhood or the neighborhood of your childhood. Imagine how these contribute to residents' worldview and behaviors.

11.3 Write a short essay describing one or more significant events in your life or the life of one of your parents. Describe how this event fits into the context of a group to which you or your parent belonged.

EPILOGUE

. . . the collective experience of other cultures sharpens the perceptions of the observer to the extent that a more encompassing humanism may permeate the observer's own civilization.

—*J. Ian Prattis*

. . . the aim of anthropology is the enlargement of the universe of human discourse.

—*Clifford Geertz*

We have read of and have thought of several reasons for conducting ethnographic research. These include:

1. to increase the general U.S. public's understanding of other cultures;
2. to improve intercultural communication;
3. to educate the public about the plight of members of other cultures (e.g., deprivation or exploitation at the hands of a national government or a world system);
4. to gain a perspective by which to develop a cultural critique of western societies;
5. to gain information by which to justify behaviors, laws, and values in U.S. mainstream culture;
6. to explain other cultures' behaviors and values using principles and laws derived from the scientific method;
7. to salvage the knowledge gained by another culture before it disappears.

This has led us to ask ourselves what reason(s) *we* intend for teaching a course in ethnography using the dialogical hermeneutic method. Our answer is complex for it relates to more than the production of ethnographies. Many students come from other disciplines and even among anthropology or sociology students, most will never produce a full-length ethnography. Yet, the course may have profound effects on them as well as on their disciplines. By learning the dialogical hermeneutic method, the students may lead a more considerate and communicative mode of interaction in their future daily life. Thus, the doing of dialogical hermeneutics may be more important than the production of ethnographies. In other words, the learned technique may be more important than the future product.

Many students, after taking the course, find that they have learned to better understand the group they study. By noticing and facing the challenges in the method, they have eliminated some of their detrimental bias. They are more empathetic to these group members, as well as to many other subcultures understood through support group discussion. They can see situations through the natives' eyes. Sometimes sympathy, defined here as an increased awareness and identification with their painful feelings, is also increased.

These processes of empathy and sympathy are especially affected because the students have chosen groups with whom they feel some discomfort. Students have commented on their increased understanding of single fathers, teen mothers, female bodybuilders, Vietnam veterans, female exotic dancers, Asian immigrants, learning-impaired adults, welfare recipients, laid-off workers, volunteer firemen, Mexican immigrants, college professors, participants in domestic violence, police officers, delinquent teens, AIDS volunteers, the dying, gays and lesbians, train tramps, and many more. Self-understanding is often increased, as well, as students begin to examine their biases, transferences, and feelings.

We hope that this was not a mere one-time experience for the individuals, but involves the learning of an approach and a posture for understanding others throughout their lives. Some students have clearly stated this. We hope that this will lead to increased tolerance in our culture, as well as to improved patterns of communication. We hope that such techniques will facilitate cooperation within a diverse community, help to resolve conflicts between groups, help in directing and counseling others, and contribute to wise leadership. Moreover, when students take these techniques with them into foreign study, they may contribute to a more global increase in communication and understanding.

Thus, when asked what we perceive to be the goal of ethnography, we emphasize increased understanding and communication within our own culture and across cultures. More specific results may be sought through application of the method to the disciplines of anthropology, psychology, and law. In the fields of anthropology and sociology, we feel that the method will support the first three goals of ethnographic research mentioned earlier. The essence of these is increased understanding of, communication with, and advocacy for cultures and subcultures. For groups that have been marginalized, stifled, or ignored, the process of hermeneutic fieldwork can prove empowering. Members will view their group as important in the eyes of a professional writer, and they will see themselves as worthy of being heard by a larger audience. This may help them to coalesce as a group, enhancing solidarity. Scheper-Hughes speaks of the element of empowerment when she writes: ". . . I believe there is still a role for the ethnographer-writer in giving voice, as best she can, to those who have been silenced, as have been the people of the Alto by political and economic oppression and illiteracy."

The type of open, self-disclosing dialogue that is sought in this method can often lead to friendships. Hermeneutic ethnographers become concerned about these informants, as one might in any close friendship. As trust and friendship builds, the field-worker may be called on to do favors for their new friends. These favors may include use of one's academic background. For example, the ethnographer might provide information about the governmental legal system, about protocol in formal situation, or about means of gaining public recognition. By providing this information, the investigator is empowering informants, that is, giving them the means for accomplishing significant tasks. In other cases the ethnographer might be asked to become an advocate for his or her informants, speaking out on their behalf to elected government officials, to human rights groups, or to social service organizations.

The important element to note here is that these acts flow from the relationships. The hermeneut is helping friends, not acting out of guilt or shame, not following a prescribed ethic. He or she is honoring their autonomy and seeking to fulfill their requests. The ethic that need be remembered is that of Kant. By treating these people as ends in themselves hermeneuts will form many close relationships and will act out of concern for their welfare.

Appendix
Helpful Hints

Students have asked to have a list of helpful hints where they might easily be referred to. We will give you such a set of basic guidelines, shortly. Although we don't recommend relying too strongly on this miniguide, it would especially help those who must leap immediately into the unknown of fieldwork.

We recommend the following guidelines for carrying out your fieldwork. However, we caution you not to rely on this list without coming to understand and appreciate the principles, unique situations, exceptions, and sequencing that the text provides.

1. *Ends in themselves.* Treat all people in your study as ends in themselves, not merely as means to an end. Be courteous, friendly, helpful, and as genuine as you can be. Be interested in who they are and in what they have to say. *Do not* treat them as mere objects of study.

2. *Open and honest.* Be open and honest with your informants. This means advising them of the nature of your study, telling them who will read your notebooks and the final report, explaining hermeneutics to them, and being self-disclosing about your own feelings, experiences, and understandings of them. Be certain to obtain their consent to carry out the study.

3. *Relax.* Try to relax during your interviews and get others to relax. "Small talk" before, during, and after asking questions of your informant (i.e., the person giving information) is one way to accomplish this.

4. *Be flexible.* In your interviews try to not refer to the list of questions that you have prepared. Work from memory on your

original questions and allow the conversation to have a life of its own. Allow the informant to have some control over the conversation.

5. *Record and transcribe.* Get down as much of the conversation as possible. This means recording, by notes or machine, your questions and remarks as well as theirs. Also, record the context of the conversation, facial expressions, gestures, etc. If you work from notes, use an improvised shorthand and add to your notes, your memory of the conversation immediately following the interview. Many students use a tape recorder and a transcription machine.

6. *Unfamiliar groups.* If this is your first fieldwork, choose a group with whom you are unfamiliar. This will help ensure that you will note differences. See table in chapter 4 for suggested groups.

7. *Contacts.* Use every available source for gaining access to your group. This could include joining a training program, giving them volunteer service, paying for their services (e.g., fortunetellers), contacting acquaintances of classmates, and so on. If possible, try to locate a facilitator—an insider who will help you to make contacts.

8. *Voices.* Ensure that all sources of variability in your population are sampled, for example male and female, young and old. If you decide to exclude a "voice" let the reader know. For example you may wish to only understand female members.

9. *Persistence.* There may be many frustrations in your research. Difficulties in finding contacts, unsatisfying interviews, and being "stood up" are among the problems you will likely face. Be persistent, and remember that a report may include the difficulties encountered along the way. Even problems represent data.

10. *Journal.* Use your reflective journal to record your preconceived notions about the group, your motives in studying them, your ongoing understanding of them, your confusion, your feelings about informants, and insights into your biases. Include descriptions of the process such as your feelings of frustration and the situations giving rise to them.

11. *Metaphors.* Examine interviews for the informant's metaphors and/or special terms. Ask for more details of these in future interviews.

12. *Challenges.* Be on the alert for information in an interview that challenges your current understanding of the group. Also,

present your current understanding to one or more informants for feedback.

13. Guiding the informant. It is proper to guide the informant with regard to what you consider to be relevant issues; it is *not* proper to guide his or her opinions on those issues.

Suggested Readings

Abu-Lughod, L. 1986. *Veiled Sentiments*. Berkeley: University of California Press.

In pp 9–24 of her ethnography, the author reveals the conditions under which she entered the field. She also relates her unique characteristics, which helped to determine the nature of her interactions. She expresses her belief that the author needs to make known the contextual details of the anthropologist's relations with the people he or she studies.

Bandlamudi, L. 1994. Dialogics of Understanding Self/Culture. *Ethos* 22(4):462–465.

This excerpt addresses Bakhtin's concept of "dialogical." His theory deals with the construction of knowledge by the self and other. This article thus describes intersubjective knowledge.

Blair, D., and I. Prattis. 1994. Exploitation in the Field. *Anthropology and Humanism* 19(1):36–39.

The authors explore the issue of exploitation and conclude that an understanding of fieldwork, based on respect, is necessary. They see the fieldwork experience as an invitation into the realm of mutually nurturing relationships.

Briggs, J. 1970. Kapluna Daughter: Adopted by the Eskimo. In *Women in the Field* (P. Golde, ed.). New York: Aldine.

In this essay the author describes how her role as adoptive daughter led to interpersonal conflict during her fieldwork. Readers may speculate on the role of transference by informants and ethnographer. Power issues, including those involved in analysis and writing may also be explored.

Brown, K. M. 1991. *Mama Lola, A Vodou Priestess in Brooklyn.* Berkeley: University of California Press.

This ethnography is eloquently written, humorous at times, and uniquely structured. The author describes her hermeneutic approach in her first chapter. Although empathetic to the native's views, she does at times enter into the scientific paradigm (functionalist and feminist explanations).

Brown, K. M. 1992. Writing about the Other. *The Chronicle of Higher Education* April 15.

The author's message in this article concerns the intimacy of relations that may (and perhaps need to) develop in the course of long-term ethnographic research. She emphasizes that the nature of the data generated is very different than for objective research.

Cassell, J. 1980. Ethical Principles for Conducting Fieldwork. *American Anthropologist* 82(1):28–41.

This article explores the issues of ethics and informed consent. The author describes three categories of fieldwork, analyzing them according to informant autonomy and the Kantian ethic.

Davis, N. 1984. Using Persons and Common Sense. *Ethics*: April: 387–406.

This article thoroughly explores the philosophical and practical aspects of the Kantian ethic. Although not related directly to fieldwork, the subject matter is in a form that readers may apply.

Dwyer, K. 1982. *Moroccan Dialogues.* Prospect Heights, Ill.: Waveland Press.

The author presents to the reader his thinking prior to each interview, each entire transcribed interview, and a follow-up analysis in each case. You will find his reflexion very insightful and his interviews worthy of your analysis. (What would you do differently?) These are good models for fieldwork and journal entries. Chapters 12 and 13 are somewhat difficult for undergraduates to understand.

Farrer, C. R. 1994. *Thunder Rides a Black Horse.* Prospect Heights, Ill.: Waveland Press.

In her short ethnography, the author uses lived experience, dialogue with informants, and refelexion to come to an understanding of Apache meaning for their sunrise ceremony, their land, the stars, and more.

Geering F. 1970. *Face of the Fox.* Salem: Sheffield Publishing Co.

In this ethnography of the Fox Tribe, the author produces an analysis using the textual hermeneutic method. Chapters 5 and 8 represent reflexive analysis by the author.

Gross, L., Katz, J. S., and J. Ruby. 1988. *Image Ethics*. Oxford: Oxford University Press.

This collection of essays addresses ethical issues in film making. These include: defining being truly informed, four categories of invasion of privacy, the political (power) aspects of informed consent, and contradictions between informed consent and "direct cinema" style. This extensive exploration of ethics makes ethnographic issues even more obvious.

Katz, R. 1993. *The Straight Path: A Story of Healing and Transformation in Fiji*. New York: Addison-Wesley.

This ethnography is characterized by a humble approach, dialogue, and the natives' understandings. In an appendix (pp. 352 to 367), the author describes his obviously hermeneutic method. He emphasizes investgator vulnerability and respect in carrying out fieldwork.

Kondo, D. 1986. Dissolution and Reconstitution of Self: Implications for Anthropological Epistemology. *Cultural Anthropology* 1(1):74–88.

The author describes her collapse of identity during fieldwork. She explains it as having arisen from the foreunderstandings of the ethnographer and her informants. From this experience she learned that ethnographic understandings are embedded in context and human relationships. She encourages ethnographers to develop experiential and affective ways of knowing.

Lakoff, G., and M. Johnson. 1980. *Metaphors We Live By*. Chicago: University of Chicago Press.

This book relates culture's metaphors to their members' worldveiw. You may find it useful for understanding how to use informants' metaphors in your analysis.

Lee, D. 1969. Eating Christmas in the Kalahari. *Natural History Magazine*. Reprinted *Anthropology Annual Editions* (1993). Guilford, Conn.: Dushkin.

You will find this article useful in illustrating the use of the dialogical hermeneutic method, particularly the appearance of challenge. It also illustrates writing techniques such as painting oneself into the picture, laughing at oneself, and event analysis.

Light, L., and N. Kleiber. 1981. Interactive Research in a Feminist Setting: The Vancouver Women's Health Collective. In *Anthropologists at Home in North America* (D. A. Messerschmidt, ed.). Cambridge, England: Cambridge University Press.

The authors describe issues of power, vulnerability, and openness that arose when they studied a women's cooperative of which they were members. Because trust could not develop without full disclosure by informants and ethnographers, the authors agreed to make their notes available for examination by all members.

Oblinger, C. 1978. *Interviewing the People of Pennsylvania.* Harrisburg: Commonwealth of Pennsylvania.

This short book is packed with suggestions for conducting oral research. Although the author emphasizes avenues for analysis of small industrial towns, many of his suggestions may be utilized for any group.

Prattis, J. I. 1985. Dialectics and Experience in Fieldwork: The Poetic Dimension. In *Reflection: The Anthropological Muse* (J. I. Prattis, ed.). Washington, D.C.: American Anthropological Association.

In exploring the ethics of fieldwork, the author recommends a dialectically engaged anthropology that would be beneficial to both cultures. Western culture's gain would be the appreciation of a more encompassing humanism.

Richards, C. A. 1992. Las Inmigrantes Mexicanas. *Journal of the Western Slope* 7(3):31–52.

This article will give you an idea of the type of report that can be produced in a one-semester, undergraduate project. This represents a good example of the technique of collage.

Rynkiewish, M. A., and J. Spradley (eds.) 1976. *Ethics and Anthropology.* New York: John Wiley and Sons.

Ethical questions have changed since this edited volume was published. However, readers may want to apply their understanding of Kantian ethics to the chapters, particularly Mann (chapter 7), Hansen (chapter 9), and Chrisman (chapter 10).

Scheper-Hughes, N. 1992. *Death without Weeping.* Berkeley: University of California Press.

Her section on method (pp. 23–30) touches on many important aspects of hermeneutic analysis: nonsolipsistic inclusion of self in the analysis, questioning of the scientific paradigm, the inevitability of bias, and the importance of interpersonal relations. Her use of the metaphor of the old-time country doctor is particularly instructive.

Thorne, B. 1980. "You Still Takin' Notes?" Fieldwork and Problems of Informed Consent. *Social Problems* 27(3):284–297.

The author explores several issues related to informed consent: When is the description of participant observation properly conveyed? Does the informant need to be reminded about participant-observation? Do some groups lack the power to grant or refuse permission to be studied? Are some groups by their nature not worthy of informed consent?

Turner, E. B. 1993. The Reality of Spirits: A Tabooed or Permitted Field of Study? *Anthropology of Consciousness* 4(1):9–12.

The author writes about her experiences in using lived experience to understand spiritual experiences of other groups. She emphasizes respect for the natives' point of view.

Twitchell, R. 1994. I Don't Even Hear the Trains Run Anymore. *Journal of the Western Slope* 9(1):22–31.

This article was written during an undergraduate one-semester ethnographic methods course. It is a good example of event analysis—a railroad company's "buyout" of their employees' contracts.

Wikan, U. 1990. *Managing Turbulent Hearts, A Balinese Formula for Living*. Chicago: University of Chicago Press.

Because she did not find what she had set out to study, the author focused on constructing an understanding of the Balinese. She describes building trust with people and experiencing them as persons-in-interaction. Her approach would be described as an ethnopsychology of the Balinese—their description of emotion, personality, identity, illness, and curing.

Bibliography

Abu-Lughod, L. 1986. *Veiled Sentiments*. Berkeley: University of California Press.

Agar, M. 1980. *The Professional Stranger*. New York: Academic Press.

———. 1980. Hermeneutics in Anthropology. *Ethos* 8(3):253–272.

Anderson, B. G. 1990. *First Fieldwork*. Prospect Heights, Ill.: Waveland Press.

Asad, T. 1986. The Concept of Cultural Translation in British Social Anthropology. In *Writing Culture* (J. Clifford and G. E. Marcus, eds.). Berkeley: University of California Press.

Babbie, E. 1992. *The Practice of Social Research*, 6th ed. Belmont, Calif.: Wadsworth.

Bandlamudi, L. 1994. Dialogics of Understanding Self/Culture. *Ethos* 22(4):460–493.

Barth, F. 1969. *Ethnic Groups and Boundaries*. Boston: Little, Brown.

Blair, D., and I. Prattis. 1994. Exploitation in the Field. *Anthropology and Humanism* 19(1):36–39.

Bodnar, J. 1989. Power and Memory in Oral History: Workers and Managers at Studebaker. *Journal of American History* 75(4):1201–1222.

Bourdieu, P. 1977. *The Outline of a Theory of Practice*. Cambridge, England: Cambridge University Press.

Brady, I. 1991. *Anthropological Poetics*. Savage, Md.: Rowman and Littlefield.

Briggs, C. 1986. *Learning How to Ask*. Cambridge, England: Cambridge University Press.

Briggs, J. 1970. *Never in Anger*. Cambridge, Mass.: Harvard University Press.

———. 1970. Kapluna Daughter: Adopted by the Eskimo. In *Women in the Field* (P. Golde, ed.). New York: Aldine.

Brown, K. M. 1991. *Mama Lola, A Vodou Priestess in Brooklyn*. Berkeley: University of California Press.

———. 1992. Writing about the 'Other. *The Chronicle of Higher Education* April 15.

Burrell, G., and G. Morgan. 1973. *Sociological Paradigms and Organizational Analysis*. London: Heinemann.

Cassell, J. 1980. Ethical Principles for Conducting Fieldwork. *American Anthropologist* 82(1):28–41.

Clifford J. 1983. On Ethnographic Authority. *Representations* 1(2):118–146.

———. 1983. Power and Dialogue in Ethnography: Marced Greawle's Initiation. In *Observers Observed: Essays on Ethnographic Fieldwork* (G. W. Stocking, Jr., ed.). Madison: University of Wisconsin Press.

Connolly, J. M., and T. Keutner. 1988. *Hermeneutics Versus Science?* West Bend, Ind.: University of Notre Dame Press.

Crapanzano, V. 1977. On the Writing of Ethnography. *Dialectical Anthropology* 2:69–73.

———. 1992. Some Thoughts on Hermeneutics and Psychoanalytic Anthropology. In *New Directions in Psychological Anthropology* (T. Schwartz, G. White, and C. Lutz, eds.). Cambridge, England: Cambridge University Press.

———. 1994. Kevin: On the Transfer of Emotion. *American Anthropologist* 96(4):866–885.

Davis, N. 1984. Using Persons and Common Sense. *Ethics*: April: 387–406.

Desjarlais, R.R. 1992. *Body and Emotion: The Aesthetics of Illness and Healing in the Nepal Himalayas*. Philadelphia: University of Pennsylvania Press.

Dumont, J. 1978. *The Headman and I*. Prospect Heights, Ill.: Waveland Press.

Dwyer, K. 1982. *Moroccan Dialogues*. Prospect Heights, Ill.: Waveland Press.

Eder, J. F. 1987. *On the Road to Tribal Extinction*. Berkeley: University of California Press.

Erikson, K. 1976. *Everything in Its Path*. New York: Simon and Schuster.

Farrer, C. R. 1994. *Thunder Rides a Black Horse*. Prospect Heights, Ill.: Waveland Press.

Gadamer, H. (D. Linge, trans.). 1976. *Philosophical Hermeneutics*. Berkeley: University of California Press.

Geering, F. 1970. *Face of the Fox*. Salem: Sheffield Publishing Co.

Georges, R. A., and M. O. Jones. 1980. *People Studying People*. Berkeley: University of California Press.

Gergan, K. J. 1985. The Social Construction Movement in Modern Psychology. *American Psychologist* 40(3):266–275.

Grele, R. 1981. Can Anyone over Thirty Be Trusted: A Friendly Critique of Oral History. *Oral History Review* 9(1):36–44.

Grimes, R. L. 1982. *Beginnings in Ritual Studies*. Washington, D.C.: University Press of America.

Gross, L., Katz, J. S., and J. Ruby. 1988. *Image Ethics*. Oxford: Oxford University Press.

Guba, E. G. and Y. S. Lincoln. 1989. *Fourth Generation Evaluation*. Newberry Park, Calif.: Sage.

Hall, C. 1954. *A Primer of Freudian Psychology*. New York: New American Library.

Harner, M. 1990. *The Way of the Shaman*, 3rd ed. New York: HarperCollins.

Harris, M. 1979. *Cultural Materialism*. New York: Vintage Books.

Homiak, J. 1992. The Mystic Revelation of Rasta Far-Eye. In *Dreaming: Anthropological and Psychological Interpretation* (B. T. Tedlock, ed.). Sante Fe: School of American Research Press.

Howard, G. S. 1989. *A Tale of Two Stories: Excursions into a Narrative Approach to Psychology*. Notre Dame, Ind: Academic Publications.

———. 1991. Culture Tales: A Narrative Approach to Thinking, Cross-Cultural Psychology and Psychotherapy. *American Psychologist* 46(3):187–197.

Katz, R. 1982. *Boiling Energy: Community Healing among the Kalahari Kung*. Cambridge: Harvard University Press.

——— . 1987. The Role of Vulnerability in Fieldwork. In *The Healing of Knowledge* (A. Schenk and H. Kaluieit, eds.). Munich: Goldman.

———. 1993. *The Straight Path: A Story of Healing and Transformation in Fiji*. New York: Addison-Wesley.

Kondo, D. 1986. Dissolution and Reconstitution of Self: Implications for Anthropological Epistemology. *Cultural Anthropology* 1(1):74–88.

Kottak, C. P. 1992. *Assault on Paradise*, 2nd ed. New York: McGraw-Hill.

Kvale, S. 1983. The Qualitative Research Interview. *Journal of Phenomenological Psychology* 14(2):171–196.

Lakoff, G., and M. Johnson. 1980. *Metaphors We Live By*. Chicago: University of Chicago Press.

Lee, D. 1969. Eating Christmas in the Kalahari. *Natural History Magazine*. Reprinted *Anthropology Annual Editions* (1993). Guilford, Conn.: Dushkin.

Light, L., and N. Kleiber. 1981. Interactive Research in a Feminist Setting: The Vancouver Women's Health Collective. In *Anthropologists at Home in North America* (D. A. Messerschmidt, ed.). Cambridge, England: Cambridge University Press.

Lincoln, Y. S., and E. G. Guba. 1985. *Naturalistic Inquiry*. Newberry Park, Calif.: Sage.

Lutz, C. 1982. The Domain of Emotion Words on Ifaluk. *American Ethnologist* 9:113–128.

——— . 1983. Parental Goals, Ethnopsychology, and the Development of Emotional Meaning. *Ethos* 11(4):246–262.

———. 1988. *Unnatural Emotions*. Chicago: University of Chicago Press.

Marcus, G. E., and D. Cushman. 1982. Ethnographies as Text. *Annual Review of Anthropology* 11:25–69.

McNeley, J. K. 1988. *Holy Wind in Navajo Philosophy*. Tucson: University of Arizona Press.

Michrina, B. 1993. *Pennsylvania Mining Families, the Search for Dignity in the Coalfields*. Lexington: University Press of Kentucky.

Oblinger, C. 1978. *Interviewing the People of Pennsylvania*. Harrisburg: Commonwealth of Pennsylvania.

Oring, E. 1987. Generating Lives: The Construction of an Autobiography. *Journal of Folklore Research* 24(3):241–262.

Ortner, S. B. 1973. On Key Symbols. *American Anthropologist* 75(5):1338–1346.

Pool, R. 1994. *Dialogue and the Interpretation of Illness*. Oxford: Berg Press.

Prattis, J. I. 1985. Dialectics and Experience in Fieldwork: The Poetic Dimension. In *Reflection: The Anthropological Muse*. (J. I. Prattis, ed.) Washington, D.C.: American Anthropological Association.

Prattis, J. I., et al. 1994. "Reflections" as Myth. *Departmental Working Paper* 94-3 Ottawa: Carleton University.

Richards, C. A. 1992. Las Inmigrantes Mexicanas. *Journal of the Western Slope* 7(3):31–52.

Rosman, A., and P. Rubel. 1992. *The Tapestry of Culture*, 4th ed. New York: McGraw-Hill.

Rynkiewish, M. A., and J. Spradley (eds.). 1976. *Ethics and Anthropology*. New York: John Wiley and Sons.

Sarbin, T.R. (ed.). 1986. *Narrative Psychology: The Storied Nature of Human Conduct*. New York: Praeger.

Scheper-Hughes, N. 1992. *Death without Weeping*. Berkeley: University of California Press.

Schieffelin, E. 1976. *The Sorrow of the Lonely and the Burning of the Dancers*. New York: St. Martin's Press.

Sherzer, J. 1989. Discourse-Centered Approach to Language and Culture. *American Anthropologist* 89(2):295–309.

Tedlock, D. 1979. The Analogical Tradition and the Emergence of a Dialogical Anthropology. *Journal of Anthropological Research* 35:387–400.

———. 1982. Anthropological Hermeneutics and the Problem of Alphabetic Literacy. In *A Crack in the Mirror* (J. Ruby, ed.). Philadelphia: University of Pennsylvania Press.

———. 1983. *The Spoken Word and the Work of Interpretation*. Philadelphia: University of Pennsylvania Press.

———. 1987. Questions Concerning Dialogical Anthropology. *Journal of Anthropological Research* 43(4):325–337.

Thorne, B. 1980. "You Still Takin' Notes?" Fieldwork and Problems of Informed Consent. *Social Problems* 27(3):284–297.

Todorov, T. (trans. by W. Godzich). 1984. *Mikhail Bakhtin: The Dialogical Principle*. Minneapolis: University of Minnesota Press.

Trotter, R. T., and J. A. Chavira. 1980. Curanderismo: An Emic Theoretical Perspective of Mexican-American Folk Medicine. *Medical Anthropology* 4(4):423–487.

Turnbull, C. 1961. *The Forest People*. New York: Simon and Schuster.

———. 1990. Liminality: A Synthesis of Subjective and Objective Experience. In *By Means of Performance* (R. Schechner and W. Appel, eds.). Cambridge, England: Cambridge University Press.

Turner, E. B. 1992. *Experiencing Ritual: A New Interpretation of African Healing*. Philadelphia: University of Pennsylvania Press.

———. 1993. The Reality of Spirits: A Tabooed or Permitted Field of Study? *Anthropology of Consciousness* 4(1):9–12.

Turner, V. 1967. *The Forest of Symbols: Aspects of Ndembu Ritual*. Ithaca, N.Y.: Cornell University Press.

———. 1969. *The Ritual Process*. Chicago: Aldine.

Twitchell, R. 1994. I Don't Even Hear the Trains Run Anymore. *Journal of the Western Slope* 9(1):22–31.

White, G. M. 1989. Stories that Matter: Narrative, Experience and History. Presented at the meetings of the American Anthropological Association, Washington, D.C. November 15–18.

———. 1992. Ethnopsychology. In *New Directions in Psychological Anthropology*. (T. Schwartz, G. White, and C. Lutz, eds.). Cambridge, England: Cambridge University Press.

White, G. M., and J. Kirkpatrick (eds.). 1985. *Person, Self, and Experiences: Exploring Pacific Ethnopsychologies*. Berkeley: University of California Press.

White, G. M., and L. Lindstrom, eds. 1989. *The Pacific Theater, Island Representations of World War II*. Honolulu: University of Hawaii Press.

Wikan, U. 1990. *Managing Turbulent Hearts, a Balinese Formula for Living*. Chicago: University of Chicago Press.

INDEX

G

H

I

J

K

L

M

N

O

P

R

S

T